Planted

By: Sharon Rose

Dedication

To the women in my life who held me up at my lowest. Their strength and guidance carried me through my darkest times.

Acknowledgements

I have immense gratitude towards my sister, Bethany, who always showed up when I needed her. Liz, for teaching me that healing isn't linear. Kasia, for showing me that I am never alone. Ashley, for reminding me of my strengths. And Melinda, for displaying grace when I needed it most.

"There is nothing more pathetic than

caution when headlong might save a life,

even, possibly, your own."

~Mary Oliver

Table of Content

UPROOTED

Deaf

What is the correlation between love and listening? I couldn't tell you. There are many who have said the words "I love you" to me, not many of them stopped talking after that.

I suppose they love the idea of me. The version I am in their heads. Once I open my mouth they don't seem to hear me.

Maybe everyone who loves me is deaf.

"I love you" are some beautiful words. Too bad they've been attached to not-so-beautiful things.

I am a human being, I have my own thoughts, opinions, and ideas.

Every time someone has loved me they've tried placing me in a cage. God I hate that. A cage, a box, a secret room. I'm expected to stay still as they carry me around in their pockets and love me.

Yikes.

It's not just one, it's all of them. Love love love, how we weaponize the word fascinates me.

No, I don't think I'll stay in line. Or in a cage, box, or secret anything; anywhere. Whether I'm blood, bound by contract, or their feelings are being shoved down my throat, if that's how I'm loved I don't want it.

Guess I'll break open the cages of love I've been trapped in. I don't find it a shame at all. I'm told there's people out there whose ears work.

And if there's no one to hear me, at least I'll be free.

Hiding Her

I lie within the steaming waters of the bath, waiting for the eruption of tears I have willfully called upon to ease my pain. Soft classical music plays from the speaker on my vanity. I take a deep breath. Exhaling, I can feel the warm stream flow down my cheeks. *Is this what it's like to let go?*

I wish to set the world on fire and walk into the flames so I can feel. *Destroy me so I can be at peace.*

He says, *"I love you."* *I love him too.* Hard to say how I got here. The bath water was still steaming on the walls. I've mastered the art of hiding, as if closing myself off has become my armor. But how can anyone reach out and touch me while I wear it?

As the water drains, making that hollowed watery sound, I step out onto the floor mat and look myself over. A hidden girl inside this woman's body is crying out. *I see you. And it's safe to come out of hiding now.*

Beautiful

I wish I could take my pain and turn it into something beautiful. Some people can create art that expands your perception.

Others can write so descriptively that you forget that you are you.

If I could reach into the depths of my soul and pull out the deepest pain I have felt, it would be a masterpiece.

Instead, I let it rip me apart from the inside. My pain is like a rock I carry down to the river so I can tie it to my ankle as I walk into the water.

It's the peace I feel when I think about the inevitability of my death. My pain is fire on a dry day. It walks towards the edge of a cliff without hesitation. I feel my pain like an ocean feels movement.

My pain has brought me to these words.

Her Hazel Eyes

Her hazel eyes stare into my soul and see only a mirror. I am an adult. *"You could fix this, you could fucking fix this!"* She sobs as she points a finger at my face when I tell her I am getting divorced. "You're not supporting me through this enough." She says to me, about this time in my life.

She refers to my *"loser friends"* and tells me that birds of a feather flock together. I am 17. She rarely sees me now, yet she still somehow manages to slice through me with her words.

She tells me she can't wait until it's legal to kick me out. I am 16. I tell her, *"Why wait?"* Pack a duffel bag and leave with nowhere to go.

She throws the office chair into the hall, a near miss as I stand frozen, I am 14. She yells and cries and screams at the grievances she's endured to raise me. Was I such a difficult child?

She stares in fright as I hold up the kitchen knife to her as she charges towards me to strike. I am 13. My hands shake, and I choke on my words.

Her eyes roll when I tell her I have my first period. I am 12. She says she has company coming, *"What a terrible time you chose. Read the directions on the tampon box,*" she says as she returns to the kitchen. I spent the rest of the night hiding in my room.

I feel her hand around the neck of my shirt as she grabs at me. I am 11. I can feel the towel rack sinking into my back as she pushes me up against the wall, my feet slightly off the ground.

She looks in awe at my peers. She says, "*Why can't you be more like her? Why can't you be more like them? What's with all this weirdness?*" I am 10.

She throws the hairbrush sharply into the back of my head for crying out in pain when she hits a knot. I am 9. "*I'll give you something to cry about!*" she exclaims.

She swings her hand across my face. I am 8. I can still feel the tears stinging my cheek as I look down at the tissues I wrongfully tried to use to clean my spilled drink.

She calls me weak. "Shall *I throw you a pity party?*" She mocks me. I am 5. I walk out the front door and hide in a bush in the hopes I can disappear.

Anguish

I melt into a quagmire of anguish. Anguish takes hold of me, grasping its arms around me.

It's almost like a blanket has been thrown over me to keep me warm. I relish in this anguish; it serves me well.

This anguish has only ever been felt in silence and alone. Where I once had to go into the back of a closet or a patch of trees down the road, I can now feel my anguish freely in the space I have created.

I remember as a small child feeling my anguish in the pitch dark, surrounded by clothes, no one could find me.

No one could tell me I was being selfish for feeling this agony or make it about them. These tears were mine, and I wanted to have them.

The warmth I could feel in my chest as water flowed like rivers down my face and neck. I took in deep breaths and exhaled slowly.

The anguish gave me relief, allowed me to feel.

In solitary is where I found my anguish. This grief gave me relief and comfort.

I sit in my space, a space that I have broken free to obtain.

My anguish gives me power and the opportunity to grow. I feel this anguish in rebellion against those who do not believe it is necessary.

Without my anguish, I cannot gain relief. Without relief, I cannot see things clearly. Without the ability to see clearly, my judgement becomes clouded. And so, the cycle continues until I feel my anguish.

I sit with my anguish, and I sigh a sigh of relief.

Sunsets

I look forward to the sunset. I imagine that it is a light show performed especially for me. The vibrant reds, pinks, and oranges put me in awe. The sunrise is beautiful with its pale yellows and light blues. But I prefer the intensity of how the sunset burns.

I smell the coffee brewing on the counter. Its fragrance reminds me of calm. I feel the warmth travel down my throat as I sip my mug, piano playing on the speaker for the house plants. I admire the Croton Mammy plant. I've noticed that it opens and closes depending on the time of day.

I hear my neighbor open and close his door and greet his dog as she barks in excitement. I listen to the crows outside my window and watch as they dominate one branch after another.

The afternoon sun feels warm, shining into my front window. Rainbows scatter across my walls as the sun shines through my crystals. I take it all in: my space, my home. All of its nuances, the little imperfections, I've grown to love because they are mine.

And like the sunset, I set out in intensity to end one day and start another. I greet the next with lightness in my heart. I will bask in however many sunsets I need to, fervent in another sunrise.

Fallout

She digs the knife in deeper. She says things that I have thought for some time now, but have not dared admit. She is my reality check, and she is angry. I can tell she has been holding this in for some time and is lashing out because I haven't been listening. Sometimes, to be heard, we must yell, and she is yelling.

She is not alone, there were others. Some were subtler, but others were like her. Women in my corner showed me sides of them that I had brought out because of my heinous actions.

Here is the fallout. The life I must repair. I tossed an atomic bomb into a city and wondered why there was dust in the air. I walked around the carnage of my weapon and questioned why I smelled dead bodies. I watched as the last building fell and asked where the shelter was.

I got on my knees and asked for understanding when I refused to understand myself. Here is my fallout. To right the wrongs and rebuild. To create a peaceful space and pray, it breaks the rubble. To hold myself accountable so I may sow new seeds into the ground. To come from the fallout better than I was.

I sow the seeds of growth into the scorched earth and hope it may begin to grow trees and cleanse the air.

Fred

Fred has made many small homes within my home. I wake to see a new thread or cluster he has left for me through the night. Fred is mysterious, only showing when he sees fit. Fred is my resident spider, and tonight, he is my muse.

I sometimes look at the way the morning light reflects off of Fred's home, which goes from my hanging Aloe plant to my window. He periodically makes a cloud in a small corner of my hallway next to my linen closet. I try hard not to vacuum it up when I clean.

My favorite of his homes has become my shower. I let the water create steam in his home and watch it shine from the droplets. Sometimes, when I am lucky, I see him there, walking the walls, moving around his legs to spin another web.

Sometimes, I wonder if Fred is alone or if he hides away from his comrades. Maybe Fred is not one spider but many, and I have named them all Fred. But either way, when I see Fred and his breadcrumbs around my home, I feel joy.

Glitter

The temperature is catastrophically low, and I can feel the burning of the cold reach into my core.

All around me is white and shimmering earth. It blankets the ground and covers the trees and shrubs.

It's as if a giant hand opened in the sky and sprinkled glitter so we may be reminded that there is still beauty after life goes into hibernation.

The muffled silence of fresh powder on the ground is an unmatched mute. And the wind blowing the bare branches is a silent symphony.

I could sit still like this forever. But then I am reminded that this season, like all, must come to an end. And when it does, I will bask in the glitter of the blooming flowers, and then the glitter of the sparkling ocean waves on a hot day, and the glitter of the changing leaves after that.

Dreams

If you shook me awake and told me, *it was just a dream*

And I looked around and realized I was seventeen; I'd
return to sleep and pray to come back

To my red carriage house on the cul-de-sac

If you shook me awake and said, *It never happened*

I'd place my head back on the pillow then, and, I'd drift
off to sleep and find myself here Where I've wished to
be on this great sphere. In my little apartment in the
center of town, Weaving my lessons into a crown.

Peruvian man

I met a Peruvian man on a hot summer night in 2006
At a hotel party. We were having some kicks. Everyone
left, and we were alone together.

It must have been the humid, hot weather.

The next thing I knew; we were enmeshed with each
other. Our clothes were on the floor, mixed with
another.

He left in a hurry before dawn arrived. I thought that
was it, another archive.

But we crossed paths again a week later, and to no
one's surprise, he wasn't a dater. That was okay; I didn't
need much.

Just a soft voice and a warm, gentle touch. The next
thing I knew; we were calling each night.

To speak to the other until the morning was bright. He
started to take me to his favorite spots.

And from there, you can connect the dots. We were in love, there was no doubt.

But we both had a lot to figure out.

The struggles began to surface on their heads, creating a divide and pulling at threads.

We moved in together, and he bought a ring. Looking back, it was an erroneous thing.

We found our comfort within our home

And Finally Decided When in Rome

We started a family, us and our boys

The house was cluttered with love and toys, and as the years went on, we became routine, Finding our happiness in between

We got to see the valleys of Peru, California, Vermont, and Mexico, too

I can't pinpoint when we lost our touch I guess now that doesn't matter much. What matters is that I remember

Everything we've been through together for 18 years was most of my life

And I spent most of it being a wife

A wife, something that I don't seem to fit, A role I was desperate to quit

And so, I left the Peruvian man to be on my own, A fear most people have of being alone

He will always hold a special place in my heart, For he was so genuine from the start

A stoic man who never faltered, Even when our courses were altered

And now I see him and feel comfort in knowing

That's because he is wonderful, and he will always be glowing. My wish for him is to find his true meaning.

Another beginning, a full redeeming.

Alchemy

I remember a time when I felt so alone everywhere I was, even at home.

From this, I learned to be solitary.

Feeling peace in the quiet, like a mortuary.

You see, I am an alchemist; I turn my pain into strength. My power raised me higher at great length.

I remember a time I was an outcast, each day at school, being harassed. Because I was different, maybe weird.

They heckled and laughed but mostly smeared. From this, I learned protection,

showing my rage as a reflection.

I remember when my heart first broke, every moment a death stroke.

From this, I learned to carry around aches and memories without astounding.

I remember when those who mattered most turned on me in a time of need.

Being their daughter wasn't enough; they agreed. From this, I learned that blood doesn't matter.

Life never serves you real love on a platter.

Love is what you find on your own with friends and lovers you've known.

Family can matter as much as you want,

but if it isn't returned, it's nothing to flaunt. I have accomplished alchemy,

for now, I carry apathy

towards those who are no good for my soul. From this, I've learned to be whole.

I Found her Head

I stood in the middle of a bustling flea market, looking to purchase something unique. It was my first time in Mexico, and I found their use of animal bones to carve out figures very fascinating.

There she was. Tall and proud, a slender skeleton woman with a long dress. Flowers around her neck and her crown. That's the one, she's the only one like her! So, I bartered with the man, my spouse arguing that she wasn't worth the sale because she had the most minuscule chip in her mouth. To me, that chip made her even more unique. It gave her character like she had lived before coming to me.

I bought her; she was mine, and I carried her around until we arrived back home, where I placed her gently on my dresser. She watched over me every day. Then I moved, and as I was packing my things, I remember placing her gently rolled in bubble wrap into a cardboard box, hoping she would make the trip to my new home.

I unpacked her in my new apartment and placed her again on my dresser so she could stare into my soul as I woke every morning. Then, one day, she fell, severing her head and sending it flying across my room. FUCK! I searched on the floor for what felt was too long to retrieve her head, maybe super glue it back on.

Several months went by, and as I still had not found her head, I resolved that she would remain headless. During this time, I experienced great mental turmoil. Not because of the missing head, of course, but because of life circumstances. I found myself on the floor of my room crying, wishing I could find my mind. And as I reached my right hand, I felt something hard on my palm. I looked down to see the small bone-carved head of my very unique woman.

Had I found her head just as I was losing mine? I realized at that moment that maybe I was finding her head now, after all these months, because I needed to retrieve my own.

I found her head! And isn't that something? Now she can look at me as my head rolls on the floor, much as hers did all those months ago. She can see the collapse of my skull as I fall to pieces. Maybe I can be super-glued back together. Aren't I glad I found her head...

Maria

In early 1900s Italy, a girl at eleven years old loses her family to a house fire, all but her little sister. She spends the rest of her childhood raising her sister on the streets of Italy. Her name is Maria, and she is my great-grandmother.

Maria was known to be fierce, even cruel. To her family, she was no matriarch, she was the devil. All my life, I've heard stories of her veracity, her strength, and her power. She held so much power, something I'm sure she learned to wield for survival.

She married a man and had a daughter and two sons then moved to America. There, in Brooklyn, New York, she raised her children in the traditional sense, with religion and family values. I wonder where she had learned these things, having raised herself? Her husband owned a restaurant where gangsters were known to frequent, and Maria was often known to hide the children in cabinets when things got hairy.

Towards the end of her life, she became bedridden, often heard calling out "WATER! WATER NANNY NELL!" and shortly thereafter died. I'm told that at two years old, I was heard yelling from my crib,

"WATER! WATER NANNY NELL!" and so the story goes that I am Maria reincarnated.

I may not have lived on the streets of Italy as a child left to fend for myself, but often times when I was met with harrowing moments, I could feel someone was there with me, as my strength. I'd like to think it was Maria, in all her cruelty, there to lend me her power.

In the face of real danger, I somehow feel a surge to keep pushing forward, without so much as a sliver of a second thought. Impulsiveness, audacity, anger, these energies that are expelled from me. Are they hers? Am I here to heal what she never had a chance to heal? Are her family wounds my family wounds?

Whatever the reason for the connection I feel with her, I know I can carry out her legacy in being a powerful woman. I imagine her at my age, her hair thick and flowing like mine, taking charge of her surroundings, referred to as mean and evil, she carries on, not afraid in the face of real danger. There will always be inside me, Maria.

Ghosts

I sometimes like to drive through old roads in my hometown, like a trip down memory lane. Everywhere I go, I see ghosts. Not the dead kind, but the ghosts of my memories.

I pass by the dilapidated homes on the north side of Main Street, a place I spent most of my time falling into an abyss. The corner store where I peed at the front door because they wouldn't let me use their bathroom, the triplex where I met my first love, that same night he stole from that same corner store and had to run from the police, I thought it was charming.

I sped past the home in which my parents raised me; I remember sneaking out of the dog door to go and meet said first love in the middle of the night until dawn broke. I pass by the hatch through which he used to sneak me in to spend the night.

I glance at his house as I relive the nights we spent entangled with each other, feeding each other's bad habits as we did. Killing ourselves slowly. Sharing every thought, we had in the process.

Then, the old strip mall where that love first told me I was his good luck charm, the beautiful, genuine smile he gave me lives forever in my memory.

I slowly rolled past the little yellow duplex on the corner, where we fed our habits and found ourselves entangled once again. I remember how he used to always walk me home and follow me around to make sure I was safe.

I drift by the stoop where he held me for too long to say goodbye, not wanting to let me go. Maybe he knew that was the last time he'd touch me. Maybe if I had known that, too, I would have stayed a little longer.

He is a ghost, not only in my memory.

Kerosene

I walk around life carrying a jug of kerosene. Lately, people have been watching me pour it out as I walk in circles around place after place. Wonder why I keep moving without lighting a match? Don't worry, I'm lighting it soon, I have to finish pouring my lines.

See, I'm scorching earth, as some like to call it. I tip the jug over and watch as the kerosene lands on rocks and splatters in different directions.

Shall I stop pouring the kerosene now? I think not. I'm not done. I have only one match; I need to make it count. I want the blaze of my fire to reach great heights and consume everything in its wake.

I finally feel the weight lift from the jug as it comes upon emptiness. I find a comfortable spot and lie down, pouring the last of the kerosene on myself. I take out my only match, strike it fast, and place it over my head.

There, I've lit it all on fire, everything beginning with myself. By the time you see the flame, I will be nothing but ashes.

Mommy

Today I had a moment I haven't felt in some time. Maybe I had to hit rock bottom to feel this desperate, but I wanted my mommy.

Before I buried her, I would sometimes reach out and see if she'd ever take that role for me. She never did.

When you feel yourself slowly fall apart, it's your mommy who holds you and comforts you; it must be nice. I've never fully understood how to hold and comfort myself, but I'd say I can do it a little, enough to hold myself up.

I cry out for my mother, but she isn't there. She sits in her rubble, a mess she's created, asking why there's a cloud of dust in her eyes.

She sets the house on fire and wonders why there's smoke. She throws a glass against a wall and wails about the shards, cutting her feet. She paints a portrait of herself and calls it a mirror.

I want my mommy, and since that is me, I suppose I'd better show up.

Stems

I just came upon a realization that I have a pretty habitual writing process. It may not seem that way because it comes off sporadic. Some days, I write for fun, and others, I write out of necessity. But no matter what I write, it always starts with a stem.

A stem, or branch, off of one of my very ordinary everyday thoughts. I may be looking at a spider crawling up my shower walls and feel myself smile and think it's worth sharing how I feel in this moment with whoever will listen, so I write Fred.

A branch off of emotion, like when I'm feeling angry, I start to watch imagery of myself in my mind of lighting the world on fire, so I sit with my laptop and I write Kerosene.

I find myself at the bottom, crying on the floor, as I place my hand directly onto the missing head of my favorite figurine. Happenstance? Or is the universe sending me a message to find my head? I find humor in the irony, so I write I Found Her Head!

And there is my writing process; I just want to take you with me on this journey we call life.

PLANTED

Pine Street

I finished placing the last of my personal effects in the double-zippered blue backpack and stormed out of the front door with it on my back and an orange duffle bag around my right shoulder. Where does a sixteen-year-old go when she leaves home? I didn't have a plan as I passed through the front door. So, I went to the center of town and sat on a rock wall next to the library for what felt like hours. I watched as cars passed, people went in and out of small businesses, and as the cold air pricked at my face, I realized that I could go wherever I wanted, that I was free. So, I grabbed my bags and started walking, with no destination. I headed west, taking backstreets, and a couple of miles later, I came across Pine Street. I had just been down this road the other day with one of my friends, and she brought me to this house that was full of people all the time. Maybe I can go there unnoticed? I rapped on the door and a guy from school answered. I didn't know him, had only seen him around, but I knew his name. He offered to come inside, and I asked if I could crash for a little while. He replied, "JUST the weekend, Sharon!" Well, wouldn't you know, I stayed for several months and became a permanent fixture there afterwards for some time. It was a wild place. There were two bedrooms and an attic, all of which housed multiple people, including me. The attic was where the guys slept, three of them all in twin-sized beds. The girls stayed in the bedrooms, I in one and two in the other. The small white house with a yellow front door, the windows all trimmed with a strange dark green, was owned by a quiet and very passive Christian woman who lived there with her son and daughter. She never had the heart to turn away a friend of her child's. I spent my days getting to know everyone in that house. We watched as some of us fell in love, experienced heartache, suffered a loss, and struggled with demons. There were regulars in and out daily, but mostly it was us, there at 2 am when everyone left, spending the last fumes of the day together. My roommates would leave plastic Barbie cups full of liquor for me when they left the house. The neighborhood was exciting, to say the least. There was High Street where the little kids would heckle you as you passed by, Summer Street where a man in a van would slowly roll his car down the road to follow you, and Emerson Street where a boy would sneak me through his window. Walnut Street, where a friend of mine lived. When the weather was nice, people used to just sit on their front porches and go from house to house. The neighborhood corner store owner never carded us, he used to sell us "loosies" for $0.50. What an interesting time in my life, living on Pine Street.

Bluffs

My brother told me some time ago that he believed that people often brought their bluffs to my knife fights. As he said it, I imagined in my mind me waving a small blade around at someone who was empty-handed, ridiculous. But I calculated his meaning by the statement and realized something. I am willing to be cruel to protect myself, at any cost, even if it's wielding a blade at someone empty-handed. My Grandfather always used to tell me, "Sharon, no one looks out for you better than you". And since I respected him more than anyone growing up, I took every one of his words to heart. Maybe that was something his mother, Maria, passed on to him. I enter every confrontation with the mindset that whoever expects me to bend for them better be willing to kill me, for I will accept death before I live a life that isn't mine. And that is my blade, I yield around the fearlessness of my own demise. I would sooner wander without a destination, with nowhere for security, then seek security in those who wish to control me. I will breathe my last breath knowing that I stayed true to myself in the end, that no one could take me and suffocate my soul. Go ahead, make your bluffs, but unless you're willing to snuff me out, I hope you're prepared for a fight.

Cicadas

There was a single large tree in the backyard of my childhood home. Every summer, the tree served as shade, something to climb, something to stare at in awe. It was massive, its branches reaching out to either side of our small yard. This is where I would see the shed skins of the cicadas. I didn't know what they were at the time, never bothered to ask. But they were the most fascinating things to me because they were left so intact that it was as if I was seeing the ghost of the bug itself. Sometimes I would gently brush the tips of my fingers against the rough shed skins; other times I would press down and watch as the skins crinkled under the pressure. I never once saw a cicada leaving its skin on the bark of our tree, never saw them hanging around afterwards either. I only ever heard them. Their high-pitched ringing sounded through my ears during those hot summer days when the air felt soupy. It was something I cherished every childhood summer, to be able to sit on the swing in the back and close my eyes and listen to the cicadas, chirping away, yelling loudly, just because I couldn't see them didn't mean they didn't exist. Now, every time I sit out on a hot summer day, when the draft is wet, and the sun blankets me in warmth, I hear the cicadas, and it brings me back to that large, lonely tree in the center of my yard. On the wooden rocking swing next to our fence, with my eyes closed, wishing the moment would never end.

Lady Bugs

I have a strange affinity for bugs, which doesn't seem like something that would describe me as a person, but I believe it says something. I regard all living things, down to the smallest of the naked eye. For as long as I can remember, I used to find ladybugs around the house and catch them with my finger by nudging them onto me. I love the way their tiny legs feel as they crawl slowly up my hand onto my arm. A funny sensation trickles up my arm from their eyelash-thin legs. Confused, the ladybug usually finds a spot and stays still. Sometimes they even use their wings and fly off me, just to hang around in the air. But mostly I enjoy placing the ladybugs into my house plants. My houseplants to them must seem like a small oasis in a vast surrounding of unnatural surfaces. There, they can feel the dirt on their feet and the leaves on their antennae, as if they're outdoors where they truly belong. Along with my resident spiders, these ladybugs grace my home and give it a small and meaningful life.

My apartment becomes a small oasis in a vast surrounding of unnatural places. My senses become aware of the minute movement, and the nature graces my home, as if I am outdoors, where I belong.

Buds

I was sitting by my picture window in complete silence. Only I wasn't in silence, there was noise ringing through my mind, my thoughts. Sometimes you lose yourself in your thoughts, forget your surroundings. Then a small sound came from just outside the window that pulled me out of my own head, a small chirping of a bird. I couldn't see the bird, but I imagined it was small, like a Chickadee or maybe a Robin, bouncing from branch to branch just outside my building. The sound reminded me of warmer days, after the bitterness of this cold finally passes. It brought me to a memory of melting snow and moisture in the air from the thaw. It reminded me that there are better days to come. Like the buds that form on the edge of every tree limb, small and unnoticeable until they bloom. They never go unnoticed to me. The buds are a symbol of growth. They appear in spring right after the coldest of days, and flower into something worth being dormant to build. Better days to come, that's what the sound of the little bird outside my window reminded me of. That no matter how cold and dark it is now, soon there will be buds and blooms shortly thereafter.

Embers

I walk around with embers at my feet

Feeling myself again is a treat

Understanding what has to be done

to make it right with everyone

Starting with my kids, they're free of blame

And their father, I owe him the same

Forest fires play their role

scent in the air like burning coal

It feels good to finally breathe

After the fire, I had seethe

The ground is cooling, I can walk again

forward towards my writing pen to finish the book, that's my story

The obscurity and the glory.

Lucid Dreams

When I dream, my soul speaks to me

It tells me things with which I may not agree

It sends me warnings through a screen

Like two worlds, I am in between

I remember all of the signs

And the truth is like a field of mines

Predictions served on a platter

telling me to ignore the chatter

My dreams show me what my third eye sees

An eye I strengthen and appease

To realize then that they weren't warnings

I've sat with this many mornings

My future was made by me alone

The dreams only prove what I had known

that I write my own life story

In the dreams, it was an allegory

So maybe my dreams don't tell the future at

My dreams tell me what I want is my call

Stacked

Maria is buried in a cemetery on a hill
Next to her husband and son at will
Next to, not on top of, because that would be strange
But her daughter lies on top, like a body exchange
Why are they stacked in the afterlife?
Wasn't her daughter somebody's wife?
Maria rests with her entire family after their lives
Except for my great uncle, he had seven wives
Please place my body on the floor
of a beautiful forest, I won't ask for more
Don't stack me in the eternity
over my unwanted paternity
Let me rot into the earth Let my body give birth
to substances that the living can eat
I'm sure my body's a delectable treat
Don't stack me when I'm gone
in a hole to never see dawn
Give me back what I'm made from
and see what beauty from it may come

Flowers

What's a Dahlia to do?

When its symmetry is off

and it starts to feel blue?

How did a yellow tulip?

end up surrounded by pinks,

It's strange to see,

So everyone thinks.

How about the roses

Their beauty is unmatched

Be careful,

Don't get attached

Their thorns are sharp and unyielding

for their protection,

and shielding

Look at the lilacs,

The purple glories

Their scent carries and tells its stories

Sunflowers face the sun

to gain its power

their heads look spun

Flowers! Flowers!

What do you see

When people look to you

for peace and beauty.

Bar Codes

I wear a barcode on my arm

I'm being raised on a human farm

I carry the same tag on my car

It moves from one to another, bizarre

My Social Security number is stamped on my head

It's had three names, with me till' I'm dead

My employee number is too long

Easier to remember if I sing it in a song

Numbers are what they see

When society looks at me

When I'm dead and gone, will it even matter

That I loved and lost, is it all just chatter

I'd like to think of my flesh and blood

not as a number but as a separate bud

On the tree of life where I stand

If yours needs lifting, take my hand

Imagine

Imagine you're standing on the road

A car speeds forward, you're soon to be mowed

Now, imagine you choose to stand still

The prospect of death feels like a thrill

What is it that makes us take risks?

So, what if I take a couple of licks

It's not like I haven't been mowed down before

called things like crazy, mean, and a whore

Stood on a highway hoping to feel

When you feel nothing, pain has appeal

Imagine I moved, just out of the way

I don't get hit, I live another day

Imagine I stayed on the sidewalk this time

I'm youthful and healthy, not yet in my prime

Why stand in the road when there's a trail over there

 Heading into the forest, it's perfect, I swear

I walk through the trees and feel a strange affection

for myself, my mind, and my body complexion

Why would I ever stand in the road?

Ever allow my worth to erode?

 Imagine I woke up and finally understood

That loving myself is the greatest good

Milk and Honey

I just masturbated and made myself tea

This is how peaceful life can be

In the land of milk and honey

I'm not trying to be funny

The air is quiet and still

I can do whatever I want at will

Now that I've left all my incarcerations

and can be in all new locations

I've gained some excitement and thrill

At the prospects I have, for this life, I'd kill

To the land of milk and honey, I go

to spend my days wearing a glow

Center Springs

There is a park in my hometown that all of us kids would frequent. It's a somewhat small park, but because the trees hid it well from the main roads, it felt like an oasis in a town that was nothing but concrete and stacked homes. Center Springs Park had a giant hill, a fountain-regulated pond, a small boathouse, and a gazebo. Every day after school, we would cut through Center Springs Park to walk home. Sometimes we would stop and meet up with people to start a Hackey Sack circle, where we would pass around blunts and catch up. Center Springs is where I once sat with an older hippie couple on their blanket after they asked me and my friend if we wanted to share a joint, listening to their life story as we sat in the dark. It's where I would go to sit alone in the middle of the day, hiding from others and gaining solace. I used to walk fast down the hill and listen to the fountain as I watched families walk through, not knowing all the deviance their children were in proximity to. We would all walk through it together, then split off to our own neighborhoods, to return the following day. What an interesting place it was. My hometown had gems like that everywhere, you just had to know where to look.

Wood Lane

I had Finally hit my limit

Got out of the life, too hard to be in it

I noticed I no longer cared

If I lived or died or even fared

I'd forget if I had eaten or even slept, body beaten

Chaos was my day-to-day

So, what if I was astray

Then one day, I looked around

In a pit so deep I'd drowned

There were people everywhere

on the floor, their bodies bare

I was living in a hole

I lost myself and my soul

to drown my demons out of fear

of admitting I got here

I took it in, all the corruption

of what life became, an interruption

I look at my friend on a mattress on the floor

and say "I'm not coming here anymore"

He laughs and says, "Yes, you will."

 "You always come back, you need this still."

I smile and nod, and walk out the door

I never went back, I won the war

Impossible Tasks

I was walking along the street, hands behind my back

enjoying the scene around me, feeling right on track

I stare at a man ahead, standing still

He stares back, my heart feels a thrill

I stop in front of him as he holds out his hand

In his palm rests his heart; it looks rather grand

He says, "Have this, it's yours, but first you must do,

anything and everything I tell you to"

I nod and agree to all that he asks

without realizing they are impossible tasks

He tells me to leave, then asks why I've left

leaving me confused and often bereft

He tells me to carry on with my walk

As he closes his palm and ceases to talk

I begin walking away from the man

knowing I did all that I can

As I get some distance away

He yells to me, "Why won't you stay?"

I know if I turn and bask

He will give me another impossible task

Women

Over the years, I've built strong foundations of female friendships, those who know how to love judgement-free and will always have my back. As I approach my 36th birthday, I reflect on how these relationships have carried me through my darkest times. There's the girl I've known since our daycare days. Like my sister, we've known each other through every stage of life. Watching our childhoods unfold. We battled the unknowns of puberty together, got each other through our first heartbreaks, and became fully mature women on different paths with the same love. The vault: She's an honest friend who has taught me emotional maturity and patience. She always has a listening and judgment-free ear and will tell me the truth even if I don't want to hear it. I can't write this without mentioning the "Sphere," which was our first group chat name. Three women I feel can comprehend my mind. We travel every year together, since they have all moved away. I consider them my soul mates, in most senses of the word. Each of them has their own strong and independent lives, and they've been my inspiration to keep working towards my goals and to never fear the unknown. The girls I just walked away from, all of whom understood my decision. They may have seen me at my lowest and still stuck around, never with any judgment. All of them are therapists in their way. We underestimate the power of strong female friendships. Women hold each other up, something that we sometimes see in nature. I will never chip away at the foundations of these friendships, for they have gotten me through unimaginable things over the years. Never knowing how to repay their love, I offer up mine, for them to have without judgment. That is the circle of female bonds.

Impulse

If I wrote an autobiography, revealing all my secrets and life story, I'm not sure if it would read like a comedy or a tragedy. Both exist in tandem like the yin and yang. The more fiercely you live your life, the higher your highs and the lower your lows. I can admit that I have had a bipolar effect on life, that most of my big decisions come to me on an emotional whim, and I take action on them. Most would say I'm impulsive, maybe even a bit mad, but I have never changed. Impulse, like when I was five and I kissed a boy out of the blue because I liked him, it was an urge. I felt such excitement afterwards, I smiled all through dinner. Or when I felt anger at recess two years later and sucker punched a boy for tagging me, leaving him winded. The sweet relief of seeing him in pain. Doing the same again when I was nine with a girl by grabbing her by her ponytail and slamming her head into a wall, with impulsive rage, she was done calling me names. The impulse to shave my head in seventh grade overcame me, making for a long hat-wearing winter. When I was fourteen, I took letters sent by my cousin, who ran away from home and hid them from the police because I didn't trust the law. How exhilarating it was to withhold. There is a brief moment in which I consider a decision right before I make it, but the moment looks something like this: Well, so what if something happens? and I carry on. And so goes the highs and lows of impulsive decision making, a decision I make purely out of emotion. Boy, has it gotten me to some interesting places, some of which I could never imagine returning. Over the years, though, I have learned to appreciate the beauty of my mistakes. Mistakes may not be the best word because everything has brought me to where I am right now, which is exactly where I want to be. So, I learn from my past experiences, both good and bad, high and low. Do I regret making decisions based on emotion? Not sure I want to answer that entirely. My life is not over yet, and there's still time to impulsively make my way through it, why not?

The Squirrel in the Attic

When I was young my cousin stayed over

for several weeks, and I got to know her

she was timid and shy, but when she spoke

it was for others that her silence broke

She had voices that told her things

she told on them like a canary sings

they told her she was being watched and deceived

I watched in wonder how her thoughts were
conceived

One day she came down from the attic

I met her gaze, and I felt a great static

she looked at me dead in my eyes

and told me there was a squirrel in disguise

he lived in our attic and told her truths

her and the squirrel must have been sleuths

because everything it told her was right, I knew

that she had figured it out, her suspicions grew

I saw what the adults were doing hiding her there

the squirrel was right, I know it I swear

Maybe her mind showed her the facts

but shifted her memory of artifacts

Her mind was fascinating, everything about it

the way she saw things, realities split

We forget the brain is an organ just like your heart

when your heart mis beats, we don't tear you apart

appreciate the mind for its complexity and grace Who
is anyone to judge anyone in the first place

Quotes from Liz

We've medicated all the shamans; they've been cut off from their higher purpose. So they can go to college, it's bullshit. You're the one who carves your path. But just know that it will be uncomfortable and cause discord. And that's just part of it, these people who think they can go through life unscathed!? You know who took life by the balls and made the hard decisions? Somebody else in this car!

If you only ever have good shit and you never have bad shit, then you have nothing to weigh one against the other it neutralizes and then your life becomes neutral. The audacity to think you're going to get through life unscathed. You think a Chickadee is going to complain about getting a small sleeping hole? Because they sometimes be roosting in old wood pecker holes. The Robin Syndrome: There's a book in the Bible that says god cares for the trees and birds, and so he cares for you. It means everything you need in the world is there, you just need to take it. If a robin is eaten by a hawk, the other robins don't feel bad about it, they're just glad it didn't happen to them. We are the only species that gets to sit there and feel bad for ourselves.

Oh, you're a limbic champion!

Forage Farm Fuck

Vermont

I sat in my car overlooking a vast reservoir that's been iced over, hitting the Blazy Susan and discussing the universe with one of my soul mates. The water was frozen over, and we watched as a couple of men snowmobiled across the ice. It seemed like a frozen wasteland, but there was something so beautiful about it. Mountains surrounded us on all sides, and the sky looked pale as if snow was about to fall. The trees were bare, and the ground was a blinding white. The wind whispered across the valley, and I listened to the silence. I used to come up here as a kid, it was practically a second home. I always saw such beauty in the untamed nature of the state called Green Mountain. My memories of coming here are different than the ones I'm making now. Family was the theme of visiting, but now I visit for me, and my experiences. We stayed at a rustic bed and breakfast. The inside was filled with exposed wood and latched doors. The home was on a hill off a main road, but it stayed quiet. It was filled with sitting rooms and books, most of which were about the beauty of Vermont, mixed with some cabin porn and nature magazines. We took a two-hour drive around the base of a Mountain near the family home of Abraham Lincoln. I believe it was the Green Mountains, what a breathtaking place! The raw and unadulterated land will always amaze me and bring my spirit back to where I belong, back in nature.

Spheres

The first time I ever attended a full moon festival was with two of my best friends. I had never been around so many like-minded people, and the energy in the building and on the property was elated to say the least. The owners of this amazing place, where people from all over can gather and appreciate art and the human experience, are well-known in the community and have been spiritual leaders through their work for decades. I watched as fire dancers flung around flaming sticks and hula hoops, and there was a bonfire surrounded by crowds of people all enjoying themselves unapologetically. My friends and I walked a small trail where we came upon a clearing, the moon shone bright in the sky, and there was a man there, alone, sitting in the clearing, in a white plastic lawn chair, smoking a joint. The definition of at peace. We went inside the home where the art lived, and music played on the surrounding speakers. There, we sat and watched as two men danced in synchronicity, so much so that you would think they knew each other. They did not know each other, for as they spoke, they asked each other questions about where they were from and how they learned to dance. How these two strangers could pass each other elegantly while speaking was beyond me. Then one of the men started to ribbon his hands through the air as if he was reaching for some invisible object, and as he did so, he said to no one in particular, "It's the spheres, man!" And something about how he said it had me intrigued. Then he repeated, "The spheres." And so, "Spheres" became the name of our first group chat. For it was whatever that man saw that night that made me remember that we are all interconnected, and forces beyond our sight exist. We are all on this giant sphere together, just figuring it out.

Wanderer

Once, when I lived on Pine Street, I disappeared for three days, and no one knew where I was. People started to trickle in after the second day to ask my roommates where I was. My roommate's answer, "She's probably out on a walk." My friend asked, "For three days?" And the reply from my roommate was, "You know how she is..." The truth was I was in a hospital hooked up to a bag of fluids, but that's not the story I'm focused on today. I was in fact wandering three days prior to those questions, as I always did. I was one of the few people without a cell phone, and I used to just walk out the front door and return when the sun went down, completely lost to everyone. I never had a destination, I just wandered. Sometimes I would go behind the Shaws to the bum trail and walk past the cities of tents, mostly empty during the day. For some reason, they always had plastic bags hung up on tree branches. I would cut through the graveyard on Broad Street and visit Maria. One of my favorite places to go was Center Springs. I would find myself in the home of an acquaintance of an acquaintance, which made them honest strangers. I went from home to home, resting on couches and eating table scraps. I would stand out by the courthouse and pan-handle, I'd tell men I needed a dollar for the bus, and once I got five, I'd quit for the day. Walking through Shaw's and eating, then walking out, was one of my favorite ways to snack in the middle of the day. It's fascinating to me that when I was in a place where I had absolutely nothing to my name, no guaranteed meal, and no steady place to stay, I somehow managed to feel the most liberated. Maybe what sets us free is the ability to have nothing. The adventure of living life and being adaptable.

Men

My grandfather sat at the breakfast table one Sunday morning and out of nowhere said, "Your father didn't want you." Geez, thanks, grandpa. What I thought he meant at the time was that my father was too tired at his age and with his current family size to have another baby, but did so for my mother. Maybe I was wrong. Most recently, an inside source told me, "Sharon, your father doesn't care about you. You need to see that". Well, what excuse am I still making for him now? Daddy issues are easy to diagnose when a father is absent. But what about when he's there? I think I'm done making excuses for the man. I've started to look at how I view men introspectively since, and here is what I've found. I have always been one to fall for the anti-hero. The guy who's a bastard, but a bastard that wants me. And that brings me to another thing. Love. Love is where I've found my mommy issues. Like when she would bring me down, make me feel like trash, then say, "I just want you to know how much I love you, and how sad this is all making me". Sounds familiar. It should be called parent issues, because we all carry them both around, present or not. And since I have psychoanalyzed my patterns with men and deduced that it's something I really should look at healing, I'll start there. Of course, I'm an adult now. I can't spend forever shifting accountability to others for my own decisions. But I'll start here, by understanding the why. Then I can begin to unravel the how, as in, *how do I break my own toxic patterns with men?*

Blue

I entered the yoga studio today feeling calm and uplifted from the smell of the thaw outside. The instructor greeted me and said, "Sharon, I love your blue yoga pants for blue day!" I stopped and thought What the hell is blue day? She must have seen the confusion on my face, so she told me there had been a message sent out to wear blue because today's class was themed. I entered the room; it was a dry 104 degrees. The playlist was also blue-themed, each song having blue in the name. Starting with Billie Eilish's "BLUE", I've been stimming on it since I left class. Having started my practice hearing the lyrics, "thought we were the same. Birds of a feather, now I'm ashamed." hit home to me, and all of a sudden, yoga became therapy. As I felt the sweat start dripping down my skin, I began to focus on my breathing. If I could focus hard enough on my breathing, I could push through the uncomfortable feelings in my body and get stronger. Then we went into camel pose. I've heard that we store our emotions in our hips and other areas of our body. Something about fully twisting my body upside down and feeling the rush of blood to my head sent me into a feeling. I'm not sure how to describe the feeling, but it was a mixture of anger and sadness, and quite frankly, I wanted to scream. What am I holding onto? I'd like to rephrase the question to What do I still have to let go of? It's all part of being in tune with your body. The body and mind connection runs deep within us. So many close themselves off to it because we've been taught to focus on arbitrary things. I am in tune with my body, and my body tells me when something needs attention, and I am obliged to listen to it.

The Orn

I find that the wisest people are those who have experienced the most turbulence in their lives. The people who face their fears to move forward with their destiny and stand and fight when obstacles get in their way. Those people are the ones I look to when I think I am alone in any struggle I may face. I was told not to write this as an inspirational piece from the one I refer to, but then I wouldn't be writing this in complete honesty; she is an inspiration. An ex-police officer from across the globe, mother of two sons, wife, and worker, these are just her identities; they are not who she really is. Who she really is is someone who has faced her own mortality and carried on. She took a giant leap to find her way forward, and after all of the bad, she turned it into good. A woman who has loved deeply and lost. She walks without judgment on others because she knows we are all one and the same. I listen to her speak on the teaching of Buddha, on learning detachment to end suffering. She is wise, and not because she's studied or listened to other experiences, but because she had these experiences on her own. She lived; she never buried her strength when things got hard. I look to her as inspiration for myself, so I may learn to live and have these experiences before my end.

42°

I'm sitting at my kitchen table listening to Carbon Based Lifeforms with my headphones on. It's somewhat trance-like in which I mean it brings me to an alternate headspace. It's mostly what I listen to when I write, if it's not classical instrumental music. I take breaks from this alternate headspace to get things done around the apartment. I've noticed something lately, I'd like to point it out. Having owned two homes in my life and established enough not to feel as if I'm missing out on anything special, people seem to pity the fact that I no longer own a home. I don't pity that fact; I quite enjoy it. Sure, someday when I can move to any location, I will find that whimsical cabin in the woods and disappear, but until then, I could harbor here forever. It's quaint and cozy, the neighbors are friendly, and they offer services for kids and families. Walking distance to everywhere in this bustling river town, the old picture window and hardwood floors give it character. The bathroom tile is just the right amount of falling apart, and the kitchen reminds me of something European. What makes it home is me and the ones I love. Having the right energy is all you need for any space to be a haven. I know, I've lived in places that look disheveled, but it somehow always felt comforting when it was where I laid my head at night. It's not what you have, it's not about attachment. It's about your energy, your regulated nervous system, and your freedom.

Madonna

Ten or so years ago, I was changing into scrubs in the work locker room, around 6 am, next to a woman thirty years my senior. We were both in our underwear, awkwardly shifting out of our pants, and I was going on about something sexual that had happened at home to another girl across the locker room. Then out of nowhere, the woman who was my senior leaned in, looked me in the eyes, and said, "You're going to sexually peak in your 50s". If I'm being honest, I was stunned when she first said it; she was, of course, in somewhat of a position of power within the institution. So, I looked at her and asked, "In what way?" She went on about how once you're of a certain age, the worries surrounding sex, and any insecurities you may have, will disappear. It will open up an entirely new world of exploring your body and everything you can do with it, with or without a partner. Having a decade between now and the interaction, I'm beginning to understand what she meant. When you are young, sex has a much more poignant meaning. We put so much pressure on ourselves and our sexual partners because we are searching for ourselves outwardly. Once you grow and experience more of life and begin to understand and face your mortality, sex becomes something entirely different. It's something we do to honor our bodies. It's the embodiment of human pleasure. Whether alone or with someone, sex should be treated as sacred. I hope to fully understand what she meant someday, and I think I'm already halfway there. Wisdom from women who have lived full lives always finds its way to me. Like the universe knows I'll use it for growth.

Wind

I always forget how windy the month of March is every year. I remember walking through a wind tunnel on my birthday to buy myself a $30 painter's rendition of "Frog and Toad" as skeletons on a tandem bicycle. The wind has been so powerful that sometimes I feel it shifting my car as I drive. The trees all dance in the canopies, and the windows sometimes shake too. Forget having a day without knots in my hair. I love the wind. It's loud and slaps you in the face. You know what else it does? It carries things to and from. The wind is one of the most underrated weather conditions. It has been known to carry sand from the Sahara Desert across the Atlantic to nourish the seas. Such a destructive force. I wonder if it knows how powerful it is. Without the wind, seeds from certain plants would never find their homes. The wind moves the sails forward and blows the dust off. Let there be wind, so we may have new air. Let the wind bring in new energies and take away the old ones. Wind, a powerful, destructive, and life-bringing force.

Green

While last week's theme was blue, today's hot yoga theme was green. I don't own anything green, so I brought my green water jug. Today's manifestations, pushing through pain to grow. I was stretching my hamstrings out, and as I felt the tug, I pulled back. Why don't I just push forward and stretch out, so maybe one day this won't hurt as badly? Yeah, why not? That's the thing about growth: it's painful. It means taking a look at ourselves, calling ourselves out for pulling back when we should push forward. Calling ourselves names, even when trying to be ironic, does no good for our mental state. Weak, pathetic, not good enough. Says who? I'd like to think that we are our own worst enemies when it comes to our personal growth. And so, I stretched my hamstring out, breathing through the burning sensation running up my thigh, and thought about how next week I will be pushing farther. The acoustic guitar plays, and the lyrics go. "Green like Spring" Spring indeed. Just like in life, I am pushing through the pain to grow. Placing my energy in safe hands and loving myself to the fullest.

But She's Your Mom

I know what you're thinking: how can she cut ties with her own mother? Here's the thing: you can love someone and never want to see them again. It takes quite a bit to find yourself in a position to feel this way, but believe me, it happens. I am not alone in the somewhat unknown group of very logical and functioning adults who chose to leave their born families behind. My father has multiple children who have done so, I'm not the first. So, what does it mean to walk away from the people who made you, fed you, clothed you, and housed you? The people who tried their best to be better than their parents, the bar was low. Let me explain how it has been so easy for me not to reopen this door. I no longer worry about the constant pendulum swings of being the scapegoat, then the golden child, a form that comes when you are alone in the home without your siblings. Both of these bear heavy weights, both are exhausting. I have accepted that both my parents are the people that they are, and

I do still love them. But I can love them from a distance. Never again will I allow myself to have such a dysregulated nervous system, especially as an adult. The behaviors may have evolved over the years as I got older and more independent, but the behaviors stay the same, toxic. Life is short, too short to be hurt by people you love.

Three Steps

I will always look three steps ahead of every decision I make. That's a ballpark number of how far ahead I look at things. Why am I telling you this? Because I think it's pertinent information for those who think I act impulsively and without fear. Here's how it works. I have a sense that something in my life needs to change. I'm not always sure exactly what it is, but I find myself feeling less and less intrigued to get out of bed in the morning when it starts to happen. HA! And there you have it, folks, the answer to all of life's problems: feed it a pill. No thanks, I think I'll keep my head. How about instead of masking my void with pharmaceuticals and pretending that the cookie-cutter facade I'm living in is real, I take action. Well, you can't just walk away from your life and expect there to be no uproar over it. This is when I look three steps ahead. Where do I want to see myself in five years? Ten years? My deathbed? No clue, but it doesn't have to be right here, forever and ever. Three steps from whatever I am is three steps further towards my happiness. Step one is the hardest, and this is why I tend to look over this and the following step, because they're steep. I leap towards steps one and two without a second thought because I haven't considered how hard they are going to be; I've only looked at step three. During the initial steps of making change, there is always a great confrontation from those who prefer comfort and complacency over the unknown potential of what their lives can be. These people usually identify with their roles in society, their place within their family, their career, and everything else that can place a label on them because they haven't done the inner work. But once you get to step three, and you're finally settled into the new life that all of the struggle and pain brought you, people turn their noses up and look at you as an inspiration. I've heard over and over from varying people that they wished they had the gall to do what I've done. Maybe not in the exact way that I did it, I don't do anything small, but in their own way. So now that I'm on the other side of causing destructive chaos in the name of change, it's my responsibility to keep being honest with myself. I wonder what my next step will be.

Overdosed

When I was 16, I broke into my parents' house and decided I wanted a vacation from being alive. Yes, I broke in. I hadn't lived there in months, and I knew they were out of town. I'm tiny, so fitting through the dog door off the basement was easy. It was a hot summer day, and the air in the house was air-conditioned as always. My mother would have never stood the heat. I had my hand in several substances back then. It was the only way I knew how to shut off my brain. I walked up the stairs to my old room, my cousin had moved into it. It looked strange, with all of his things scattered around where I used to spend most of my days. I don't remember how much of what I took, but I do remember having the goal of a coma in mind. I didn't want to die, at least that wasn't the initial thought. I felt myself start to fade. Getting up to go pee, everything going black, waking up on the floor. Repeat, repeat, repeat. I had hit a low in my life. I felt alone while surrounded by people. Maybe I did want to die, I know, at minimum, I didn't seem to consider it a risk factor to what I was doing. I must have had a sliver of life left in me because somehow I managed to call for help. Next of kin was my sister; she's always been a stand-in mom. The nurse watched me writhing in pain and said, "You did this to yourself." What did she even know about what I had done to myself? My parents came, brought me back home to recover. I was clean for a week before I went back, met my first love, and dived back into it again with him. It wasn't until a year later, the day of my sister's baby shower, that I decided to stop once and for all. Being sober for her was more important to me than anything, and somehow it stuck. I don't regret my past decisions, only because I have learned from them. I am grateful to have moved forward, and with me I carry my weight, and it makes me stronger.

Days

I woke up today to the sound of small bird chirps outside. I noticed the air looked misty and began opening windows. The fresh air hit me, and as the fan moved it around my apartment, I began to feel a sensation of peace wash over me. Such small things can put us in good moods. I showered, dressed, placed headphones on my head with the tune of Carbon Based Life Forms, and headed out for a walk. I stepped out of the building and was hit with the scent of damp ground; the clouds covered the sun just enough to shade my eyes. I crossed the street and walked side by side with an elderly gentleman who commented on my hurried pace. I took one ear off my headphones to listen to him, and replied, "I'm just hurrying by." He smirked, and we both carried on. Cars flew by in a hurry, and people walked their dogs along the sidewalks surrounding the grocery store plaza. The store was bustling with people, some grabbing full carts, others small baskets. I only took one item out with me, Lion's Mane Mushroom Coffee. Entering the threshold of my front door, I was hit with a wall of warmth after being out in the cold. I started brewing the coffee, and as the scent filled my home, I decided I wanted to start a new book. There are several books on my shelf that I have not read. One in particular is a book called "Hiking Through: One Man's Journey to Peace and Freedom on the Appalachian Trail" By Paul Stutzman. I bought it at a gas station in Vermont about 5 years ago. In the Prologue, he talks about leaving the comforts of his life, his job, his home, to go on this journey to heal. After losing his wife to a terminal illness, he did what he thought would comfort his soul: he set out into nature. I like this book already. Days don't have to be filled with anything in particular. They can just be simple. What makes up our days are the moments we have with ourselves, and sometimes with others. Why not keep having days, different as they may come, I will take all of them.

Gloria

She was 18 when my father was born. Growing up, I thought 18 was old enough to start having kids, so I never understood what the big deal was until I reached that age. My grandmother Gloria was an eclectic woman. She had a French-Canadian heritage, speaking the language until she stopped using it in adulthood. She would have never been caught knitting or hugging her children. She birthed seven children, with five surviving after the first day. She didn't bother naming one of the children who died, so his grave reads something like, Baby Boy. Her husband, my grandfather, was an avid drinker, and it eventually ended his life. Once, when he was drunk, he lit their trailer on fire, stepping outside while she was still in it. I don't think they had a good marriage. When I was 15, she visited from her home in Georgia and brought me her old lingerie, she didn't have any more use for it, so she figured I would. On my 18th birthday, she sent me a card with a check for $25 that said, "Thank god you're

18, now I can stop sending you cards- P.S. split the money with your niece." All of her children, four sons and one daughter, except one childless uncle who moved to Thailand, have a detached parenting style. What I mean by this is that they do not have close relationships with their children, and it seems to be just fine with them; this was how Gloria was. One went as far as living on a boat to avoid back child support payments. In her old age, Gloria found love again in a man named Charlie. She said his name with an accentuated "chAAHHHHHLAY! He called her "My Pixie". Geez, more than I needed to know. She was in tune with her sexuality well into her 80s and always prided herself on how attractive her children were. The older I get, the more I see Gloria not as a grandmother or a mother, but as a woman. I wonder if in her youth, she wanted to just go off into the woods to be alone and feral, collecting men along the way. I never really got to know her; she wasn't one to come around family much. But I think that had she been around more often, we would have had plenty to talk about.

Maybe I'm Weird

Today is the perfect solemn day. It's cloudy, rainy, yet warm and cozy. So naturally, I went to visit Maria in the graveyard. I arrived at her grave and took a good look around at the quiet scene, and noticed that she had gained a new neighbor.

There it was, a fresh body in the ground, the dirt newly packed around it. I considered lying right over the smooth dirt, then decided my coat wouldn't recover from the wet mud. Instead, I went into my car trunk and pulled out a plastic bag, then walked over, took a big chunk of graveyard dirt, and placed it in my car to bring home.

Maybe I'm weird, but I do somewhat envy the fresh body in the ground. Finally, being able to rest and become one with the earth seems peaceful. I laugh when people make idle threats about harming me, as if I wouldn't make sure they pointed right between my eyes and didn't miss.

I am weird because I just don't see what the big fuss over life is about. Aren't we here to just enjoy the ride? I find amusement in my daily life listening to people go on about arbitrary things. Live, Laugh Love? More like Forage Farm Fuck, as my friend Liz would say.

And what are we even here for? To have a nice vehicle, a constant house project, an overdue tax bill, overtime, and a headache? No, I think I agree with the mound of dirt I hovered over this morning, that can't be it. I'm here to breathe, as long as my lungs will let me. I am here to see, as long as I have eyesight. I am here to feel, as long as I still have nerve left. I am here to love, as long as I still have a heart.

Phenotypes

I am of Italian, Irish, British, and French-Canadian descent. If you were never to have known that, and you looked at me, you would see a woman standing at average height, about 120 lbs, long, thick, curly, mousy brown hair, slightly tan skin, and expressive facial features. These are my phenotypes; they are not who I am but how I look. I have my father's mouth and my mother's nose. My hair correlates with the Italian in me, and my long, thin legs are from the French. What does any of it matter where my looks come from? It doesn't matter; what matters is how I see them. I spent a lot of my younger years trying to change my phenotype to fit what I thought was the standard of beauty. As I saw myself age, the idea of being someone else lost its touch. I began to see the way my hair went wild when left in its natural state, I saw my eyes as a beautiful color of Amber, I watched my body in the mirror as it showed me its wisdom. Every person's body has a story. It is a combination of everyone who ever came before you, and the story of it shows your personal history with it. I like to look at people's bodies and read their novels. We all started invisible to the naked eye, and here we are in a form that allows us the privilege to walk this earth. Every cell in your body is an imprint on the earth, yours is unique, yet so much the same as everyone else. My eyes, your eyes, may not be the same color. We may have different amounts of melanin in our skin, and your body may be vastly different than mine inside and out, but we all share our differences. What an oxymoron it is!

The Ugly Side of Human Nature

When I was 12, I was at a hotel with a group of my peers for a martial arts competition. On the off hours, we went down to the pool. There, a girl on my team who made it her job to ostracize me swam nearby. I'm not sure what came over me, but all I remember was feeling red-hot rage, so I took her by her ponytail and submerged her head underwater.

Naturally, her arms started to flail around as she desperately tried to come up for air. I was essentially killing her. She used her sharp nails to scratch at me, but the adrenaline rush kept me from feeling it, and the harder she fought, the tighter my grip became. I could feel my eyes widen and my fist clenched so hard I thought I might break my fingers. She was at my mercy, and it felt good.

It took someone intervening to undo my fist from her hair and finally allow her to come up to breathe, my arms were covered in defensive scratch marks. Had we been alone, would I have killed her?

This is the uglier side of human nature. I have found myself capable of great harm when acting out of emotion, especially when I've allowed something to build up. I may not have ever come that close to killing someone like that since, but I have done my fair share of paybacks that have landed me in a lot of trouble with a lot of people.

Do my primal human instincts take over the logical, more developed side of my brain? Am I capable of one day snapping again and losing my head when feeling threatened or just plain tired of taking nonsense from people?

The court system tries murder differently when there's emotions involved; a crime of passion is what they call it. So it's understood then that human beings can reach their limit and lose themselves to that little reptilian brain we all still have.

Getting older and emotionally maturing means you know when the anger serves you, and when it doesn't. Learning to let go of things that do not serve you and letting karma work on its own time is the cleanest break you can make from someone who invokes anger from you. Walking away with your head held high and leaving them to their own devices keeps you at peace.

No one is safe from the uglier side of human nature, but the more we look at ourselves and understand our uglier sides, the more we can learn to use them to our advantage instead of our obstruction.

Sunlight

Ever feel the sunlight and wonder how

You would ever think to allow

anything to bring your spirit down

or submerge you until you drown

I can't think of a single thing

In this moment, that would bring

any negative emotions

I've already cried oceans

Winters come and winter's gone

Spring is here like a newborn fawn

Springtime to my life, I mean

All I see around me is green

This new dawn is bright and clear

All I know is I'm still here

Air

I smelled the freshness

Warm summer days are coming

My windows are all open

WATERED

I Wrote About You

I wrote about you when I mentioned the breeze

I thought of you when I watched the trees

The sunlight warms me, and when

 I used to think, *wonder how he's been*

I held such love in my heart

I never wished us apart

 My feelings were always real

I went through a lot to heal

 The hardest part was opening my eyes

To all of your deflections and lies

Forgetting I was a person with a soul

You tossed me into flames like coal

used to keep your fire warm

Seemed to be my only form

I don't think love does those things

Looking back, it truly stings

Her Purest Form

I sit in the backseat of my mother's blue Honda Civic. She turns to me with a smile on her face and says, "Shar, I can make the light turn green watch, One, Two, Three, Presto Chango!" I stared in awe as she waved a finger, and the light immediately turned green. Now every time I am at a red light, I watch as the other side turns yellow, then red, and in my mind, I say, One, Two, Three, Presto Chango! She used to sing the chorus to Crocodile Rock constantly, she's the only reason I know every lyric. It was our song. Beneath all of the projections, anger, self-pity, and rage, she was human just like everyone else, still is. She never thought she was good enough at anything, which would explain why she picked up expensive hobby after expensive hobby to fill the void of feeling like she didn't have talent. What came from these things were amazing scrapbooks, her ability to hem anything, a knack for computer language, and an eye for Celtic housewares. When she would laugh, her voice would reach an ear-piercing decibel, her eyes would squint shut, and she would lose her breath. Her sense of humor surrounding just about anything was the core of her friend's entertainment, and she always loved screaming loudly during rollercoasters and horror films. I remember sneaking into her bed as a child when I was scared, she would awake to see me and gently place her arm around me as we slept, the most comforting thing she ever did. How could someone like that be so toxic? I don't think she's ever loved herself. It's not just that I witnessed my grandfather and great aunts belittling her constantly, her closest relatives never pulled their weight, and she became the scapegoat. What happens when a girl is born into a family already riddled with children, a violent and exhausted father, and a judgmental Irish catholic mother? She is put down, beaten, told she needs to change her appearance so a man will want her, called fat, stupid, and unlovable. No wonder she settled for my father. Had she done the work of peeling back the layers of abuse in her childhood, she would have found that someone like her is in fact worthy of love, but first, she has to love herself. I don't know when and if my mother will ever realize that inward is the direction she has to start. I know that under all of the gaslighting, manipulation, and animosity towards me is that little girl who waited for someone to show her love. I tried to show it to her, but I can't be her mother, and I can't be her father. I can't even be her daughter. Her healing is up to her, and mine is up to me. I can only wish that someday she finds the love she should have been given as a child, because quite frankly, I think she deserves to feel it.

Painted Sky

The clouds were placed over the pale blue sky

by a painter with her brush and dye

Brush strokes are softly placed

 Not a single edge misplaced

It's what god made so we can feel

 love, cherish, honor, and heal

The painter knows her place here

On this living, breathing sphere

Reds and pinks over the horizon

She paints what her soul lies in

She steps back to see her creation

The bigger picture brings her elation

Namaste

Yoga was themed with the color red this afternoon. Rose colored heart shaped glasses were handed out at the front desk, so I threw a pair on, *why not*? Once the glasses were on, everything became a tinted version of the color red.

Was this an analogy being thrown in my face? Of course it was! Everything around you is the universe speaking to you. Most things in the studio are, in fact, *not* red, but from where I was standing, everything was. It was the heart-shaped glasses, *go figure!* It made me laugh out loud at the irony. Aren't we all a little blind to true colors when we look with our hearts?

I sweat more than usual today, leaving the heart-shaped glasses on just to amuse myself all throughout class. The sweat poured off of me from everywhere, and it was like I could feel all of the negative energy leaving my body.

At the end, we lie on our mats and the instructor says a final word. Today, it was something along the lines of, "We are all in charge of our worth." Then we said our *Namaste*, which translates to "I bow to you". The class repeats the saying, and we all bow to each other verbally.

Something about the way in which she said her last words made me wonder if she knew a thing or two about what I have experienced recently. As I walked out, I chatted with her and she said, "As you know, healing is never ending, there's always something to work on." She was speaking my language.

There is something to be said about people who surround themselves with others on a healing journey. It's good to know that there are those out there who can show me the way.

Silent Sister

There's someone who's been present in my writings but never mentioned until now, my sister. When I was born, she was 15. She'd carry me around with her friends and tell strangers that I was her baby. How ironic that she has been the motherliest to me during this time in my life. Daddy's little girl, an unsought title she was given at birth, is the glue that keeps whatever remnants of her family together. She just wants peace. Her calm and passive nature makes her the easiest of us to be around; she's kept most of her opinions to herself. My silent sister, who's never yelled, patronized, or belittled, had a lot to say this year. She must have practiced patience with me more than anyone. Always answering the phone with a listening ear, my sister has guided me through the depths of strife. When I first made big life decisions, she sat back and watched, as if she was preparing to catch me if I fell. When I needed to hear hard truths, she showed me a side of her I didn't know existed. It came purely out of love. I hope she knows how grateful I am for every two-hour phone call, every visit, every rant, and every rave. I will always remember the genuine support she's given me and the unconditional love she's shown me

The House

When your neighbor's television plays so loud it shakes the building, you pretend you're at the movies and imagine you're walking past one of those IMAX theaters that rumbles the floor beneath your feet. I sleep under most conditions just fine when I'm tired enough. Although my downstairs neighbor doesn't share that sentiment, as he has knocked on my door over the noise above his head, my bad. The lady next to him plays guitar and sings in a band. She's pretty, on top of that, surprised I haven't seen her bring a man home. Wonder if she feels the same about me? She threw a dinner party once; I could smell the wine and garlic from the hallway, sounded lively in there. The dog next door, owned by the man with the IMAX theater, wakes up early and demands a walk around 6 am. He leaves his front door. I'm pretty sure he's the only one who uses that entrance. That's not true, actually, I use that door when I go for my walks. And it's where our mailboxes are. I wonder if they think any of these things about me. Each one of us is living in the same building, yet knowing nothing about one another. Aren't we all in our little bubbles?

Quiet Noise

I walked along the edge of the road near the Green River Reservoir. It was Mid-July, some years ago, the sun was strong, and the scent of my pheromones intensified by the sun hitting my skin. I was alone for as far as I could see, and the silence was anything but. I heard the Earth speak to me. First, the wind came down softly and whispered through the tall grass, "You're not alone, I am all around you." I watched as the sea of green moved and took in a deep breath. Then the crickets began to sing as if to say, "there's joy in the little things." As I carried on my walk, I came upon an open field. The cows were feasting as if I weren't there. Then one looked up at me and stared, her eyes asked, "do you know where you're headed?" I turned onto the dirt path leading to my family's home, high up in the hills of Vermont. The path is dark under the canopy of trees. Once you enter, the temperature of the air cools about five degrees, and you can feel it instantly. The shift in the air declares, "things may change in an instant." I make it to the clearing, back to the house, and look upon the miles of mountains on the horizon. The mountains are vast, majestic, all-encompassing giants that assert, "you are but a small part of this being."

Earth Bound

"Nasa Astronauts Speak out after returning to Earth"

reads the header. I'm serious, for what it's worth

 Imagine saying "Hey, man, how has Earth been?"

I wouldn't even know how to begin

"Oh, you know, not bad, just a few things

Just a war or two, all men think they're kings"

How do you answer honestly?

"Well, love is now an anomaly"

I don't even watch the news anymore

All it shows is the broken, starving, and poor

Walk outside and look around

We are all still Earthbound

A Declaration of Love

Sometimes I walk around looking at what's on my bookshelves and randomly pick something up and turn to whatever page opens. Today, I grabbed "Your True Home," The everyday wisdom of Thich Nhat Hanh. The random page it opened to: A Declaration of Love. It reads: "What is loving? It is recognizing the presence of the other with your love. This is not a theory; it is a practice." It goes on to say that whoever you're loving doesn't matter, it is all the same; Dear one, I am here for you. Love as a practice, I took a minute to think about this after I read it. Love as a practice. How many people have told me they loved me and never practiced it? On the other hand, how many people have said they loved me and practiced it? How many people have I said I loved, and how many times have I practiced it? When we take an approach to love as a practice, it forces us to see who puts actions behind their words. I know. You'll be disappointed to look back and see quite a few people who never practiced what they preached. But maybe that's why looking at love as a practice can help us weed out the liars. A common saying is that actions speak louder than words. Sounds like the same concept with love. I've experienced acts of love from those who have never spoken the words to me and felt none at all from some who claimed to love me deeply. Love is the gentle touch of a friend when she sees you're hurt. Love is the person who shows up for you when you're in the most need. Love is always there when you call, without judgment or fear. Love is lifting each other up and walking along the journey of life side by side. Love is actions, not words or great declarations.

Love is a practice.

Among the Trees

When I feel like hiding from the world, I walk among the trees

The trees don't ask me what is wrong, or why I'm hiding

They don't expect an explanation or solution

They let me be, almost as if they are not there with me

But they are very much there with me

They provide the seat in which I perch

They bestow shade so I may keep my eyes open

They keep me covered from the rest of the world so I may disappear

They show me that growth takes time and is well worth the wait

I wish to live and die among the trees, for they have been my dearest friends

Do you remember 1942?

I just stayed awake for longer than I would have liked, it's okay though, because I signed up for it. But yesterday, was it even yesterday or was it the day before now, I sat in the back office catching up with a man I've known for 15 years. He said to me, "Hey Sharon! You remember 1942?" How on earth could I remember nineteen forty fucking two? I shot back a confused look, like he had gone mad, or at least madder than I recalled. He laughed and said, "That's what I thought! You were fine, and so was I. Because we weren't here. And guess what, you'll be fine when you're gone too." I can't argue with the man, how could I? He makes perfect sense. Where was my consciousness before March 3, 1989? Somewhere in the ether, I would imagine. Or maybe I was stardust, just floating around waiting for a force to drag my particles into a form and force me into this body. What a body it is. It's weathered every storm so far and lived to tell the tale. It's been ripped open in every sense of the word, and put back together, the ends never meeting the same again. Someday, I will be wrinkled if the universe chooses that for me. My hair will be a shade of white or grey, my agility will slow, and eventually I'll be dead. My body will be dead, not me. I'll float back out there, to wherever it is souls go when they're done here. I wonder if I'll ever get another body, or maybe I'll go on to some other dimension, ethereal plane, or just into the dirt. Who cares, because honestly, I cannot remember 1942.

Fred is Dead

I've known for some time now that my resident spider, Fred, has not made an appearance. His lifeless webs have started to fall off the walls, and as I was cleaning the apartment this morning, I decided that it was time to vacuum them up.

How long do we hang on to the remnants of something that we know is never going to return? I would have liked to think Fred would have said a final goodbye, or at least leave some friends for me to keep his webs alive, but no.

I guess that's part of grief, learning when to let go of the remnants, the reminders, and the memories. The hardest to forget are the good ones, because we like the way they made us feel. The hardest to let go of are the bad ones, because they remind us of our pain, and why we left in the first place.

I guess I'm not talking about Fred anymore.

A coworker of mine wrote a book about two married people who fell in love. I read it many years ago. It was a tragedy, go figure. I never asked if he had written this from personal experience, naturally, everyone had their speculations of where the book originated from, but I think it's best left unsaid.

I suppose I knew when I fell in love in the manner I did when leaving my spouse, that it would end in heartbreak. I don't dwell on the why, or whether or not the experience was genuine.

In his book, my coworker mentions his character cleaning his house, he comes upon a spider web. An internal monologue follows, that he doesn't want to disturb the spider because the spider causes him no harm. I remember telling him after reading his book that part of the story stuck with me. He found that a bit odd, but it's what I thought of when coming upon Fred's final web in my home all these years later.

It's the small things we remember. Something that may hold no meaning to anyone may mean everything to you. And when I saw the last remnants of Fred, I thought, *it's okay to say goodbye even when there's no one to receive it.*

SPROUTED

Life Goes On

The raven blinks and just for a second

I see the whites of its eyes like death is winking

It waves hello and smiles at me

I wave back because we're old friends

Sometimes, when the sky is grey, death speaks to me

reminds me we have a date, and I cannot miss it

When the moon is full, and I can see clearly at night

Death shows me what's in store ahead

like a vision of the future

I Am

This is my home

It is wherever I am

There is my joy

In the moments I have

There is my heart

In the ones I love

There is my soul

in who I am

There is my entity

an ethereal being

There you are

Just as you are

Here I am

just as I am

Ms. Rose

A man at work recently started referring to me as *Ms. Rose*. And *Rose* finally reflects everywhere and has officially become the only name I am known as.

This wasn't a name I was given at birth or retrieved in my marriage; it is one I chose for myself. The idea started when I decided I wasn't going to keep my married name, I didn't like the idea of having any attachments to a man. But the idea of going back to my maiden name irked me.

So, I googled how to change your last name in my state and printed out a checklist. I wasn't sure what I wanted my name to be, but I knew I wanted the change. Then a friend at work mentioned the name *Rose* and how much she liked it, and it seemed to stick.

I sat on it for a while. I said it out loud a few times with my first name, *Sharon Rose, Sharon Rose*, and decided, what's in a name anyways? Why not have a name that I claimed for myself? Most of my life, I've been strapped to the vehicle of someone else's expectations. This name is mine, and I want it to say, *no one owns me.*

Ms. Rose. I hope I will honor the beauty and strength of the flower itself. I hope I get to see the outcome of this journey, I'm thrilled at where it may take me. I've come this far already. If anything, I've just gained momentum.

Advanced Directives

People do the most outrageous things in the name of *love*. Love will make you forget who you are, believe in hopes that will most likely never come true, and love will selfishly keep you alive against your will. This is why I've written an advanced directive.

Yesterday, the father of my children stopped by for some paperwork, and while I was in the cabinet, I decided to hand him my advance directive. After the initial shocked look, he tried to cover up his face, I explained.

The person in charge of me when I cannot speak for myself is a good friend of mine, she knows who she is. The directive states that under no circumstances am I to be kept alive on any support systems in the event of my body being unable to heal itself from any occurrence. I do not wish to die in a facility, instead, I wish to be removed, taken into the woods, and allowed to go in peace. I demand to be in charge of my own death.

I now have this in writing. When I cannot speak for myself, it is those who "love" me who will intervene and do what they think is best for me. More like, what they think is best for themselves. Selfishness has always been a trait in those whom I call *family*. Like Munchausen by proxy, there are those who would make my ailments their own, including my death.

At what point am I allowed to have agency over my body? When is it okay to tell someone that their illusion of love for me doesn't give them the right to take away my autonomy? If they had their way, I would sit in a coma on display until I rotted away, forced into a crematorium or a metal box, to again be on display. I am not a display item.

Another advance directive section places me in an unmarked grave. I do not wish for those who knew me in life to know my whereabouts with the exception of my POA and my children. I cannot control whether I live in someone's memories or not. What I can control, what I hope to control, is my body's return to the Earth, the way it was intended.

In the name of *love*, there are those who would stop me.

Shook

A firefighter and a nurse walk into a bar. They never entered a bar; the nurse doesn't even like alcohol. They walked upstairs. How cliche. Thought it would be a good pseudo start to a joke, but we'd be the only ones laughing, I suppose.

I'm sitting on my couch listening to Jimi Hendrix radio, naturally, he plays, then others like him do. "You Shook Me" by Led Zeppelin is currently on, there's a long instrumental, and something about this music, and the way my curls look barbaric this morning has me feeling some type of way.

What is it about autonomy that makes me straighten my back? What is it about having regency over my body, my mind, and my peace that brings me so high that nothing in the world could bother me at all? I'd like to think this is what it feels like to breathe.

Who needs a bra when I can throw on a halter top and be just fine? Who needs all those hair tools when what my hair looks like on its own is intriguing and free? I have a lot to smile about, but mostly I have myself.

It's been nine minutes and Robert Plant from Led Zeppelin is still singing *"Ain't you never been shook?"* Oh yes, I have indeed.

The Burning Tree

I first moved into my apartment in the early fall. The trees were all green, and I didn't know which would show the brightest colors when the air turned cold. When it finally did come time to see their color show, one in particular stuck out to me.

It is settled in the back of the parking lot, a medium-sized tree with unimpressive bark. Its branches shoot out and make the top half of the tree look almost circular. In the fall, the leaves stay green at their root and turn blood orange from the middle out, it's really a sight to see.

Every day I would leave for work in the early morning hours and look over to see if the moonlight would illuminate it enough for me to appreciate the colors. In the afternoons, the sun would hit it just right to make the tree look as if it were on fire. I was constantly in awe at the warmth that came from that tree.

After the leaves fell and winter came, I sort of forgot about the tree of fire behind my building. It blended in with the rest of the trees. But earlier today, when I arrived home, I looked over at the burning tree and saw that it had started to bud.

Tiny little green pods are coming out of its smallest branches. It reminded me of the fire in which they go out. A final fireworks display, a goodbye show when it's their time to fall. They start just like that, tiny little light green buds at the end of a branch. How peculiar to already be thinking of their bright, fiery, burning death.

The Heart Soon Follows

On January 1st, I wrote a piece called "Beautiful" in which I described my pain as being so deep that if I were to turn it into art, it would be a masterpiece. It's true, I was constantly struggling with misery and uncertainty.

When I wrote this piece, I had in mind one person. *Be careful what you wish for.* I wish I could shout that from the rooftops now that I'm on the other side. But we all tend to have some desires in life that we know are not aligned with reality.

I haven't written about my sorrows in quite some time, probably because I haven't had many.

I used to pretend that the greatest source of my agony at the time was the falling out with my parents, or my divorce. But it was actually from something I had wished for. Something I had asked the universe for; someone I thought I wanted in my life. Looking back, I must have thrived in denial. Funny, that's the first stage of grief.

I guess subconsciously my true self was calling out to break free from the toxicity, not sure why I fought it for so long. My heart wants to stay, but my mind is strong enough to pull me away. A survival mechanism of sorts.

When I observe, listen, and engage, there comes a great understanding. The first to accept it is my mind, and the heart soon follows.

Coffee Table Books

Some days, I wander around my little apartment and just admire my surroundings. I walk with my cozy winter socks on my feet, so thick they could be slippers. Pacing isn't uncommon, and I usually stop to admire my coffee table books.

They're mostly large hardcover books that hold photography of nature, information about trees, mushrooms, and the universe, and I love randomly flipping through them.

Did you know that beefsteak mushrooms appear to bleed, with blood-like latex commonly dripping from the mushroom as it grows. The Lobster mushroom is a rare parasitic mushroom that takes over another mushroom as a host and covers it with pink, orangy film.

Bald Cypress trees grow directly in swampy water and are the state tree of Louisiana. Flowering dogwood reminds me of a place I used to sit around and do nothing most days, This tree is known to grow at the forest's edge.

I'll sit and flip through the photo book from the Hubble telescope, although I'm sure they have much nicer pictures from the newer James Webb, guess that's my next Coffee Table Book Purchase.

Oh, I forgot what I was doing. That's what happens when your mind wanders around the apartment. Guess I lost myself in the bookshelves, the plants, the smell of dinner cooking, the sound of my children playing in the next room, the sound of my life.

Roof Tops

While living in the lively and very odd neighborhood surrounding Pine Street, when I was 16, I made friends with a girl who lived in a little White, red-trimmed house on the corner of the main road. Her family was familiar to me; I heated up one of her older male cousins' Camaro often when I had an animalistic urge. They weren't just a family, they were townies.

Known for their long beards and Harley-Davidsons, a classic car in each of their driveways getting rebuilt, I envied them. My friend and I used to go out of her second-story window and climb up to the roof. We'd lie ourselves out and just sit there for hours talking and watching the world around us.

I attended many of their family cookouts. I knew the kids by name and age and found myself at home with them. Not sure what it was about them, maybe it was the way in which they were so unapologetically themselves.

They gave a new meaning to family for me. Sure, every family has their issues, and no one is perfect. But I always admired the families that knew about each other's flaws and made them simple facts about them and moved on. Those summer nights on her rooftop, listening to the sound of cars driving by, and her parents sitting in the living room watching television together and laughing, gave me warmth.

Turbulence

He's in the sky, gliding beautifully above me. A wingspan that impresses in size. Hawks are beautiful, strong apex predator birds. *Oh, what just happened to him?*

The hawk dips sideways as the wind goes against his wings, as if he is tumbling in midair. Like a human tripping on a flat surface, the hawk tips back and forth, trying to regain its control. Even the strongest of us have our weak moments, but the hawk eventually regains its flow.

Turbulence is something we have no control over in life. That's probably why anxiety exists: we think we are in control. The hawk does not fly high in the sky at breathtaking speeds and worry about the changes in the wind.

He would never consider falling from the sky, instead, he glides with the flow. What makes us stronger is how we handle the air when we hit a disturbance.

When you see someone suffering, in struggle, do not view them as weak. They are just regaining their footing and correcting their course. This life we have is connected to everything, a constant shift, movement, and flow. Turbulence is a chaotic change in flow, not the end of it.

Honor My Death

Earth is a being. If you put your hand under a microscope, you'd be surprised to see what looks like mountain ranges, the ridges of your hands. We are all just small parts on this being we call Earth.

I am alive, the definition being that I have animation and means to communicate with the rest of the living. What about after our deaths? Does the being not break down and store my compounds for other things? Do I not live through the trees, the sea, and the breeze?

Tell my children that I am not gone. I am still a member of this being, in a different form. Tell them not to mourn me, but to look into their eyes and see mine, tell them to listen to the wind and hear me, remind them to touch the earth and feel me.

Recycled energy is what we are, on this living, breathing planet. This expanding and shifting universe. cosmic entity, we forget we are all a part of.

Crown of Thorns

According to the New Testament, a crown of thorns was placed on Jesus to mock his claim of authority. I wonder if it took away his authority. I suppose, since there is a holiday commemorating his death, I would say not. Self-proclaimed authority, such as claiming a connection to the divine, is not exclusive to the man who we know as Jesus Christ.

All of us, in our way, grasp our connections to the divine, whichever divine it is you choose to follow. Spiritualism has become a new and rising practice among younger generations. The elders of old tribes and secluded places still carry on old traditions from when humans were closely connected to the Earth. The *neo-traditionalist,* let's create the name for nomenclature's sake, understands that we are moving farther and farther away from our natural states of being.

So, is it not fair to say that if we are all interconnected to this planet that gives us life, we are all equally connected to the divine? Some people find their way to it through church, dogmatic religions, being in nature, praying to old gods and new, and arrive at the same altar. The altar is life, death, and everything surrounding it.

All of us walk around wearing a crown of thorns, with our self-proclaimed importance. We are not only connected to the divine, but we are also part of the divine. Jesus may have been the son of God, but we are all created from the same orbiting life force. Let us never forget that our lives are sacred, from the poorest man to the richest. Every mother is equal in her ability to bring life, every child is capable of growth. We are all divine.

Rainbows

It's the first hot day of the year, and my son and I walk around the grounds, taking in the brushed-stroke sky. I've opened all the windows to invite Mother Earth back into my home. Still, I hear the humming of air conditioners in some of these units.

I've waited for this, and as I walk by the row of trees blossoming pinks and whites, I can feel the life breathed back into my chest.

A rabbit comes out from underneath the bushes and offers us entertainment for a moment as we pass him by. His eyes follow us as he chews on grass. The sound of children playing in the courtyard echoes out, and the cars driving by create a stream-like flow of white noise.

The sky is pink, then gradually it becomes a burning orange. The clouds are wisps across the sky, and there is a rainbow forming over the houses at the end of the road. I stop and stare at the rainbow, and I hear my son say, "That's beautiful". *Yes, it is, and so are you.*

I thanked him for joining me on the walk, and he replied, "I'll probably come again next time." Well then, I look forward to it.

The Resurrection

Today is the day the resurrection of Jesus Christ is celebrated. It couldn't possibly be that this is also the time of year that we celebrate the resurrection of the life around us. Nature is in full bloom, and the sun warms the ground, thawing the last hold of winter.

This is the time of year that the windows all go open and I allow the air to flow through my home, the sound of birds in the morning, and crickets at night, like I'm living outside. It is also the time of year I deeply cleanse my living space and deeply cleanse my aura.

There is a lot to cleanse off my aura this year, and already I feel lighter. My path's been redirected, and there has finally come a clearing. I can see that this path doesn't lead me off a cliff. It seems to be leading me into a garden.

Funny how life works. It's hard to see where you're going in the dark. Then the sun comes out and shows you that there is life all around. It sometimes even sheds light on you, and you become visible to others.

The Universe wants you to stand in the light before you accept love from others; it wants you to love yourself first. It wants you to become resurrected, so you don't have to carry the darkness you left behind into the garden you are entering.

Mellow Beauty

A woman is a sacred being, a fact no one can deny. Religions and governments have placed rules to keep us *"protected"*. Ancient wisdom viewed the feminine as divine and influential. And in modern society, people still fight to protect the sanctity that is womanhood.

For a woman to be in her eternal energy, things have to align. In nature, our bodies sit like sculptures, something to be cherished. A man who can bring about his side of the duality between the masculine and feminine creates balance. To feel safe brings us into our mellow beauty.

As women, we forget these energies; most of us are hardened by the expectations to uphold both ends of the divine. But when we find ourselves surrounded by a strong male force, we begin to let ourselves flow naturally back into womanhood.

This does not mean that women are not capable of maintaining strong masculine energies, but something changes in us when we are at peace. We begin to let things go, unbothered by the energies of those outside our sacred circle, we tend to regulate our nervous systems and bring calm to chaos.

Let me be in my feminine energy, even if just for some time. Let me be one with this serenity that is inherent in my natural state. May I bring calm to whatever chaos comes my way. I am here in my half of duality.

The Founder's Bridge

When I was a kid, my mother would bring me into work and leave me in a room full of computer servers with a book or activity while she plugged away at her cubicle. Her co-workers would pop in and have small conversations with me throughout the day.

The server room was hot, the fans all loudly blew like white noise. I used to find it so peaceful being left alone in those rooms, and the visitors always broke up the silence with inquiries and offers. Some would offer me snacks, others would bring more paper materials, it was like being at camp.

Every time I'd go to the office, we would drive over the Founders Bridge, one of only three bridges crossing over the Connecticut River into the capital city. "Welcome to Hartford," it reads, with pride. Over the years, it's earned some of that pride, becoming a city of more than just a bad reputation.

I used to read the engraving as we would pass under it, and know we were close. Close to the warm room with the white noise, and the large open cafeteria, which had mannequins hanging from the ceiling, I always wondered why those were there. I sometimes wonder if they still are after all these years.

Some memories are beautiful, even the ones that weren't surrounded by much joy. Some memories are quiet, like our minds were in those moments. This is one of my quiet memories. One that brought me peace, and the peace is what I remember every time I read "Welcome to Hartford" over the Founders Bridge 30 years later.

Bus Stops

I sit on the curb, soaking in the sun, waiting for the school bus to arrive at the bottom of the street. My kids live in this neighborhood half their time. I used to live here too. A figure makes its way towards me, and I can make out that it's my father.

He chooses to stand across the road, *not sure why we both have to be down here*, then he finally turns to me. "The bus will be here any minute". These are the first words he's spoken to me in months, and I'm not sure how to respond.

Could it be that he feels comfortable speaking with me without watchful eyes? I give a small smirk and nod my head, it's all I can muster up at his statement. Then there's an awkward silence, as if this was the conversation starter he'd been waiting to use, then he turned his back to me and faced the road, arms across his chest in silence.

He's a tall man with a thin body composition. Approaching 80 years old, I know his time here is becoming more and more limited. He wears khaki pants and a button-up shirt tucked in. He looks frail.

I can think of a few other things he could have said, but it seems as if we both were at a loss for words. As the bus pulls up, we both walk towards the corner, and when my son gets off the last step, he looks back and forth between the two of us, amazed that we are sharing the space. The walk home was silent.

I sometimes wonder how much the children understand, if at all. I'm no longer carrying around anger, sadness, or despair. I've moved on from wanting to witness karma of any sort, and I genuinely want to keep my peace. But small moments like this make me question whether they have done the same, or not.

I wish I could have told my father *I love you.*

Truth Seeker

Friend keeper, oath breaker

Free bird, soul shaker

Are you a truth seeker

Signs in the sky maker

Sun rises, moon falls

One day, the truth calls

Tug tug, pull pull

Spirits stay with you still

Books and Covers

Just skin and bones, I'm wearing baggy sweatpants and an oversized T-shirt, and I'm in pain. I look just like a drug seeker. I find myself *sitting, standing, sitting, standing, crying.* The emergency room staff stare, and when the nurses take me back, they give me a sad and almost pitiful look, as if I'm somehow faking it. I try and distract myself by writing "Truth Seeker" from a small, hard armchair.

I'm wearing the wrong cover. Several hours later, I'm taken to a stretcher in a hallway surrounded by rhythmic beeps, and the smell of urine and coffee combined makes me want to live in my shower. I notice a girl behind the main desk, who recognizes me. We went to nursing school together.

I watch as she steps over to the Emergency Room Physician, and all of a sudden, he notices I exist. He walks over and asks me to recount my day and my symptoms, then asks what I do for work. What an interesting question to ask someone writhing in pain. "I'm a nurse," simply put. *And no, I am not who you thought I was.*

Looks are deceiving, this is why I never judge. On the other hand, who are we to judge either way? Turns out I wasn't faking, and wouldn't you know, they gave me the strongest pain relief, treated me, and sent me home with instructions.

I work in the field, my patients come from all backgrounds and ways of life. They are all human beings. Funny how much we can dissociate from treating others equally. I thought about the way in which the demeanor changed all around once it became known I wasn't some junkie off the street seeking a high.

Short of showing up and announcing what I do and how I live, there is no way of avoiding outside judgment. They see my cover, but they haven't read my book. I hope that all my fellow healthcare peers understand that this is the case. Pain strips away our pride and our dignity, all of us.

Maybe the more we live, the more we suffer, the more we can appreciate our health, and the experience we call the human condition. Don't allow yourself to become trapped in the notion that one human experience is more valuable than another; that's when we find ourselves trapped in judgment.

The person rocking back in forth in pain is you, in another form. Someday, it may even be you in your form.

Waters

Choppy waters rock the boat

swing, sway, swing, sway

Am I nauseous yet? I am

clouds above me, dark and grey

brace for the storm coming this way

rain comes hard, pours over me

Now I'm clean, now I'm free

There's the sun peeking out

a warm welcome without a doubt

Loosen my grip on the rails

Relax now, open the sails

The wind will take me

to where the sun shines

I hear the water softly push

Against this boat I've built

love for who besides myself

invites love in from somewhere else

Thank the universe for my pain

It's made me stronger

It's made me gain

water pushes and water pulls

My sails move forward

And I'm still here

UnKept

I am the sand sifting out of your hands

Returning to the sands of my land

I am the water leaking through the walls

Returning to flow with the stream below

I am the wind blowing through the city

To move the waves on the open sea

I am unkept, I cannot be caged

Some have tried to their dismay

I am the air seeping out of your jar

To be free and floating, not where you are

I am not owned by any man

I am a woman free to follow my plan

GROWTH

Love

I don't know what love is if I'm being honest. I don't think anyone has come up with a definition to fit everyone's standard. Maybe we're all confused. But there is something I am learning to do, and that is to love myself. Whatever that means.

I am flawed, no doubt, very. I have made many ripples in peaceful waters. I suppose that's my way of kicking up the dirt from the bottom to see what surfaces.

I am curious in nature. I like to see where the road less taken takes me. I have always danced to the beat of my own drum. I am not afraid of failing, because I know I'll always get back up, and if I somehow don't, at least I know I tried.

I guess maybe in a way that is loving myself. Loving myself by allowing my soul the experiences it craves, loving myself by leaving places that dampen my aura. Maybe all of the hard and painful decisions I have made, all of the struggle and hurt I had to push through, were self-love.

It is self-love to walk away when I know something is not meant for me. It is self-love to go through torment so I may let go. It is self-love to remember who I am, the girl who left home without a plan, the woman who left home without a plan. And here I am, still standing.

Love, I suppose it means staying true to myself, whatever that means.

The Being

This morning, I ventured into the expansive state forest in my town. As I drove onto the very unkept dirt road, I felt as if I were entering the mouth of a great giant being. The trees are alive, they breathe in tandem with us. They are the yin to our yang.

Respect this being, and it will protect you. The forest doesn't care who you are, what walk of life you come from, or how much money you make. It cares that you enter in peace. It wants you to leave the way you came, and always remain in balance.

I left my car on the side of the narrow dirt road and started walking up the steep trail.

I could hear the wood pecker stabbing into a tree from a distance. The smaller birds sang in harmony to one another above my head in the canopies. The greens sprouting off the branches were light, baby in color, and in nature.

One tree does not consider itself an individual. It lives among the forest of its kin, such as we are to one another. We tend to forget this. I am honored that I may enter such a massive and symbiotic being. One wise and harmonious entity. The forest, the being, where I wish to rest my head.

Post Apocalypse

People speak of the end times being right around the corner. I hear it all the time. *"Start preparing for the downfall of society."* My grandfather once told me he lived through many end times, each of which entertained him greatly.

There was Y2K, 2012, and the possible third world war we face daily as we look at the news feeds. So, what does it matter if you're prepared for the end times? Wouldn't you rather be dead?

Hard to tell if I'm being funny, *I'm not.* I haven't watched the news; everything I know about the world around me is word of mouth. I walk outside my door every day knowing a comet could crash into the earth, a flash of light and a mushroom cloud could appear, a bus could drive right through me.

Shall I live in fear? Maybe storing away some canned goods will make me feel like I have some control over the situation. One fights nature when they prepare for life on a planet that would not sustain them.

Idiocy! While I'm enjoying my final moment, my spirit finally at peace, there will be those fighting to stay in their suffering, out of fear of the unknown. That's what it is really...the fear.

Well, if you must *live in fear*, then do so. But please don't ask me to join you.

Silence

I sway back and forth in the wicker swing chair by the open window. The storm clouds roll in, and I watch as the wind starts to pick up in the trees.

The apartment has just been cleaned and I'm taking in the silence. I didn't choose this silence, one of my children chose it for me when they snuck into the living room and turned off my speaker.

Guess they're tired of Stevie Nicks. But they did me a favor.

Thunder starts to boom in the distance, and I decide to turn off all the lights and light candles instead. I love a beautiful thunderstorm, especially when I have such good seats to it.

My plants will miss the afternoon sun, and I'll miss the light show of the sunset, but it's something new for a change. It will ring in the air like an orchestra.

My picture window is the theater, my silence the orchestral pit.

The Faceless Man

When I was seventeen, I was sleeping with a Colombian man. He was handsome, at least that's what people remind me of him. It's been almost twenty years, and I cannot remember what he looked like.

He has no social media, and the last time I bumped into him, I was in my twenties, and it was brief.

I remember his car, his apartment. I even remember details about our intimacy, but in my memory, he is faceless.

How can I have shared moments and my body with someone, and not remember what their face looked like? Strange that my brain can do that. I sometimes wonder if it's a mechanism to forget.

When I walked away from him, he struggled to let me go, I suppose history does have a way of repeating itself. But why can't I remember his face?

If he were to approach me today, I'm not sure I would know who he is. And that is life.

One day, everything you've ever done will be just a memory. There is no guarantee that you will ever remember someone's face, their body meshed with yours, the places you've been, the sounds you heard, the things you felt.

There's no guarantee greater than everything ending. He is the faceless man, one who doesn't even live in my memory, because I can no longer conjure his face.

But still, I hope he is well.

The Allegory

I was reminded of Plato's Allegory the other day, the one in which he talks of leaving a cave, seeing the light, and never being able to return to the cave. An analogy for never being able to go back to what you've left behind, after realizing the truth.

When he said it, I couldn't believe how accurate it was for how I had been feeling about my life lately. I left a cave, although it didn't feel like one while I was in it. Or maybe it did, and subconsciously, I knew I had to step out into the sun.

I almost feel like I'll wake up from this dream, this freedom to walk the path I'm most compelled to do. Growth is painful, but I'm more afraid of not living. I'm fearful of ending my days with "what if" or "who am I".

Maybe I have stepped out of only the deepest part of the cave. Maybe I still reside here inside, but closer now to the light. My vision has become clearer, but have I fully stepped outside?

Teachers

Today's theme at yoga was the 80s. Perfect, they have the best hits. I've been using my practice to think. The deeper in thought I am, the less I feel the stretches and pulls of the poses.

Today's thought: My Philodendrons finally like me! I've always connected with Pothos, but now I have two varieties of vining plants growing like constrictors around my apartment.

Ever since living on my own, my thumb has become greener; must be the peace my plants feel in their new atmosphere.

Bon Jovi sings, "It's my life, it's now or never. I ain't gonna live forever. I just wanna live while I'm alive." Yes, thank you, Mr. Jovi. I agree with the verse.

My instructor creates the theme every week, and her playlist speaks right to me. I let my hair down in class to let it breathe. I feel free as it sways back and forth in camel pose.

We are inspired by teachers. They could be anyone; it doesn't matter what their degree is on paper. I am taught by those who love themselves and know how to love others; this makes them teachers. I learn from my mistakes and share my lessons with others, which means I am also a teacher.

Oh, the lessons!

Cheers!

What if I had never changed the course of my life? I know I'd be daydreaming about living it while sitting under a tree pretending to be someone else, *how sad*. Oh well, I suppose I'll do what I set out to do, why waste the opportunity?

Writing as a hobby has been nice, I wonder where it will take me. I daydream still about the life I'm heading towards, but now there's nothing in my way. Curious how taking life into my own hands has worried so many people. *I'm entertained.*

What will I think of next? Guess I'll think of it while deep in thought, one of these Sundays at the farmers market, *I can't wait for that either! Cheers*! to whatever happens in five minutes, or an hour, or tomorrow, or next year, or the rest of my life.

Home

Liz hung up the last of the frames on my apartment wall. She and our close friend had spent the last two days trucking what little I had left from my house into my new space in early September. This was it, my new home.

She went to leave, and we stood in the kitchen and held each other and cried. She said, "You did it, you're free." As if I had escaped some sort of prison. A prison of the mind. I broke away from a long life of being held onto by others, and at the time, I didn't realize I wasn't finished cutting people off.

She walked out my door, and as the door closed, I stood in my kitchen in complete silence. I was home. First thing I did was grab a 500mg cube of psilocybin and christen every room on my own. Then I paced for a little while. Then I cried.

Every journey begins somewhere. Most are born from the dismantling of the last. Had I dismantled everything for nothing? The answer to that is an astounding, *No.*

Growth is painful, scary, and hard. All things that make you stronger. I left an 18-year relationship, and my parents and I became a hidden commodity, which seemed mad at the time. Looking back, it still seems mad.

The road was long, steep, bumpy, and well worth it. Being on the other side of madness is refreshing. I wish I could go back and tell myself the outcome of this would be okay, but then I'd never put in the work and learn the lessons.

The journey's not over. Not even close. And thank god for that!

Sunshine

She sits up like a cartoon character, typing away

Her head bounces up and down, and she's smirking

She's always smirking these days, how very odd

Another day of watching the fire brigade bring the heat

He calls her "sunshine" as he leaves

She's been lit up since this morning

away she goes to ponder how she'll smell the roses

It's almost that time of year when she'll be lying out on her blanket

The sun hits her skin and warms her from outer space

Listening to the sound of the birds and the wind blowing through the trees

How funny life is when it reminds you how alive you can feel

Like, there was never a storm blowing through you not long ago

There's the rainbow after the rain

And the sunshine has dried the earth

Everything Small

Write about leaves instead of flowers

Write about twigs instead of trunks

Write about small nuances in your life

The smell of your coffee brewing

The way the light illuminated the floor

simple surroundings and nowhere to be

Your memory brought on by a scent

The way you feel when you take your first step

towards something meaningful

And open your eyes to everything small

that has made everything big

Soft Rose

"Burning Hour" by Jadu Heart plays over my speaker. *"Take another breath, you're all out of time. Body in the flame burning in the fire."* This time last year, I was in the Outer Banks having an existential crisis over what I thought would be the end of my marriage; turns out I was right. What was I so afraid of?

A few weeks later, I had a vivid dream about being stuck behind an old station wagon at a four-way stop; no one else was there but me and the old car. The wagon sat idle while I looked around at what the pause was for. The dream became my reality for several months. Rebelution plays in "Fade Away": *"You and I are one together, I know this won't last forever."*

Guess I'll go around the wagon.

Add it to the playlist of my life. The album has gone through changes since it first started, and yet somehow has come full circle. Florence and the Machine take over now with "Dog Days are Over": "Happiness hits her like a train on a track."

What if life is just a series of albums?

It's a stark difference from the Weekend's takeover some months ago of "Baptized in Fear." *"Trying to right my wrongs, my regrets filling up my head."* Dark times for the playlist.

Through it. It's the only way to grow.

Each journey has its beginning and end. You don't seem to notice the end of one until you see the beginning of the next; they all run into each other. Makes sense that Lisa Hall made her way back with "Is This Real?" *"And I know, yes, I know, but is this real?"*

Define real.

The playlist is ever-changing. An indicator of the road I'm taking and how it has moved me, just ask the music. Hippie Sabotage sings, "Until I'm free, I'll behave like I'm immune to danger. I cannot sit in one place: it's not within my nature."

Throne

I once sat on a throne I called my home

It was a great deflection, maybe a projection

For all I saw were bars and chains

Leaving sometimes entered my brain

Little did I know my mind was working

At getting me out and never returning

I was fearful and hesitant

But my mind would not sit in it

Then the universe gave me a mirror

Some things I started to see clearer

I saw myself and where I was headed

If I didn't take back my life, I would dread it

So I burned down my throne

Watched as it went up in flames

You can't have fire without pain

I now have a throne of wisdom and truth

It sits in the ashes of what I went through

It's made of my struggles and fears

Surrounded by a moat of my tears

This throne goes wherever I go

It is the lessons that helped me grow

Pyres

Where there's smoke, there's fire

The flames burn higher and higher

I look forward to being set ablaze

Heat moves through me like waves

It's sundress season, how exciting

To walk around in this weather is so inviting

Let there be sunshine and markets and fires

Burn my old life in the pyres

Sunshine beams illuminate my skin

In this new life I'm in

Pinks

I just stopped dead in my tracks to look at the sunset. It's baby blue with slashes of pink, *how beautiful*. I've thought about what the trajectory of this piece would be, but I'm at a loss.

I've just stopped to take a picture of the newly formed purple cloud above the pinks. I'm observant in nature, *and in nature*.

That's why I realized something about myself, on Mother's Day, as I walked around the main street of my hometown. I know every dark corner of that town, not because it's a *bad town,* but because I was looking for them.

What a wonderful distraction it was to bury myself in the grievances of society so I may lose sight of what coming home felt like. Then maybe I'd forget and want to return.

I walked and walked and walked and finally realized *it was never this town, it was me.* I wanted to hide in the dark corners behind Main Street, and off North, the Econo-Lodge, and most of the west end.

Center Springs, the bum trail behind Shaw's, *I think it's a Save-a-Lot now*, various residences of people whose parents either didn't notice or didn't care if another child squatted in their home. I was good at hiding.

The purples in the sky have sunk, and the dark blues are coming out to welcome the night, *mesmerizing.* It's doing this over my hometown, too. *It's nice not to be hiding.*

Swings

I don't like to dwell, but I'll be honest, sometimes I do. There are a handful of things that have happened during my time on Earth that I can't seem to shake. Here is one of them.

The last time we spoke, I remembered feeling rage towards him. Even over the phone, I knew he was trashing his body and fading away. The slurred speech, repetitive, and inconsistent thoughts. I knew he was the same, and it killed me.

We were so young when we met, yet we had such adult ways of living, and not the good kind. It's hard to remember exactly how we bonded, through trauma, I'm sure, and that never ends well.

I spent countless nights sleeping under the warmth of blankets on his bed as he spoke every thought in his head. He always snuck me out of his house in time for his mother's alarm clock in the morning.

He'd pop back up in my life unexpectedly as if the universe wanted me to look at him. And look at him, I did, *all of him*. Maybe it's easier to say how I feel now after finally grieving him. I had held onto his memory for so many years that it had become exhausting.

I rocked back and forth outside on my swing, holding the phone to my ear as he spoke every thought in his head, *like he always did,* and he told me, "Sharon, you can do better." I was sure at the time he meant my husband because he then asked me to go for coffee, but now I wonder if he meant himself. Neither of us knew this would be our last conversation.

Looking back, he spent most of the conversation apologizing and telling me how great I was. I thought he was blowing smoke up my ass. The next day, he texted "I'm sorry," to which I never responded, and he died shortly after.

It's one of my greatest regrets. I spent over a decade loving a man and never telling him because I was mad at him. I was angry at how he lived his life, and how I lived my life alongside him. What would have been the harm of telling him he was loved?

Driving Ms. Rose

I got my first white hair. Not grey, no. The brightest white. I was excited. I have always imagined myself as one of those old women with blinding white hair down her back. Grey is nice too, but I'm glad I got the former.

If I'm lucky enough to keep sprouting whites from my head, then maybe I'll have lived long enough to see where this all takes me. To the grave, of course, but what about before then?

I am the driver of my vehicle.

People would say I am not the safest driver. They would be right. My seat is always a little too close to the wheel, my head a little too far back. I speed through yellow lights, sometimes red ones. I play my music loudly over the speakers, and the seat heat is always on for my back.

And this past year, I spent most of my time off-roading. So many bumps. The high highs and the low lows just kept on coming. What else did I expect when choosing the unpaved road?

I wouldn't have traveled down any other path.

Who knows, maybe there will be a couple of greys sprinkled in there at some point. I'm sure it will be beautiful either way. My vehicle moves on towards its final destination, and before then, I'll be looking at the road ahead.

Enlightened Energy

The air is soupy; it's early on this hot June morning. I'm walking to Starbucks. I'm a glutton for a dirty chai tea latte. My headphones are playing a mix of Hozier. His music reminds me of slow summer nights by a fire. Smelling the burnt wood is soothing.

I hate to say it, but I'm glad I committed homicide last year. I buried and mourned who I used to be. There was always something inside me desperate to shine through. The old me had to die to let her out.

I walked past an older couple, and the woman smiled at me. I could feel her happiness seep into me, like walking through a pocket of warm air in the cold. These are the things that I want to write about. The aroma of freshly ground coffee beans fills the air as I enter a bustling atmosphere.

This is my new life, so far. I have no idea where this road will take me, if I end up anywhere at all. It's the journey I'm still on. I've found myself taking my armour off and feeling connected again.

I found a verse in a book, and was intrigued to save it for a later conversation. I watch the sun set, setting the sky on fire, from my swing chair and take a photo so I may send it overseas.

Who are these strangers all around me, becoming less distant by the day? I know it's coming, the next event of my life. Let there be more; they always push me forward. "Enlightened Energy" by Hippie Sabotage plays on the speaker, and for a moment, I forget I'm sitting on my couch sipping on a dirty chai in my home. In this life. In my ever-changing story.